T0135747

Efficient Algorithms for Structuring Wireless Sensor Networks

Olga Saukh

2009

Angefertigt mit Genehmigung der Mathematisch-Naturwissenschaftlichen
Fakultät der Rheinischen Friedrich-Wilhelms-Universitt Bonn.

Erstgutachter: Prof. Dr. Pedro Jose Marron, Universität Bonn
Zweitgutachter: Prof. Dr. Kurt Rothermel, Universität Stuttgart

Datum der mündlichen Prüfung: 21. April 2009

Bibliografische Information der Deutschen Nationalbibliothek

Die Deutsche Nationalbibliothek verzeichnet diese Publikation in der
Deutschen Nationalbibliografie; detaillierte bibliografische Daten sind
im Internet über http://dnb.d-nb.de abrufbar.

ISBN 978-3-8325-2244-5

Logos Verlag Berlin GmbH
Comeniushof, Gubener Str. 47,
10243 Berlin
Tel.: +49 030 42 85 10 90
Fax: +49 030 42 85 10 92
INTERNET: http://www.logos-verlag.de

Acknowledgments

Writing a dissertation takes a long time and involves contributions and support from many people whom I would like to express my sincere gratitude to.

First of all, I would like to thank my supervisor Prof. Dr. Pedro José Marrón for the opportunity he gave me to do my research in the field of wireless sensor networks. I am thankful to him for the freedom I had in exploring my ideas and working on the subjects that I really care about. I also wish to express gratitude to Prof. Dr. Kurt Rothermel from the Department of Distributed Systems at the University of Stuttgart. I had the pleasure to spend the first three years of my PhD work in his department and I am very thankful for all the support I received during that time.

There are many people in the Sensor Networks and Pervasive Computing Group at the University of Bonn and the Department of Distributed Systems at the University of Stuttgart who provided interesting feedback and valuable suggestions. I would like to say thank you for that! Additionally, I would like to send a virtual thank you to the Gaggle and VSDSL computing clusters for working very hard days and nights to finish my simulations in time!

During this work I collaborated with my colleagues and very good friends Robert Sauter and Matthias Gauger whom I hold in high regard. Thanks for supporting and criticizing my ideas, always taking time for long and often late discussions and also for an important discovery I made: Some of the best ideas come around 3:00 a.m. and if the deadline is at 5:00 a.m., then there is a good chance that the paper is still submitted well on time.

I wish to extend my warmest thanks to all others who have helped me with my work. Among those, I would like to mention Vladislav Duma who I thank for checking the correctness of my mathematical proofs. I also would like to express special thanks to Oksana Tymchyschyn and Alexander Schaeffer for improving the readability of my writing and for supporting me during the whole time of my research.

During the work on my PhD, I had the pleasure to participate in the two very interesting European projects "Sustainable Bridges" and "Aware" that not only provided financial support to fund my work but also contributed motivation and ideas for my research. I would like to thank all project partners that I had the opportunity to collaborate with. I would like to express special thanks to the partners from AICIA in Spain and from EMPA in Switzerland with whom I worked very closely in my research.

Finally, I would like to thank my parents and my brother Alex for their love, belief and encouragement in all my professional endeavors. I am deeply grateful for the huge amount of support and inspiration they give me! I feel it every day of my life wherever I go and whatever I do!

Contents

Contents

8

List of Figures

List of Figures

List of Tables

List of Tables

Abstract

A number of application scenarios benefit from using wireless sensor networks for monitoring, tracking and event detection purposes. Since sensor nodes are small and energy-constrained and possess severely limited computational capabilities and memory resources, sensor networks require the development of a new generation of algorithms targeted at large-scale networks, unpredictably changing environments and constantly changing network topologies. Thus, self-organization, adaptation to dynamic changes and generally a higher degree of distribution are essential characteristics of these algorithms.

Structures appear as a result of self-organization of the nodes in the network and are defined in terms of the cooperation between individual nodes. Many sensor network systems require constructing structures in order to perform correctly. Popular structures are trees, groups and clusters, partitions and boundaries.

The contribution of this work is twofold: First, we analyze, evaluate and classify structures and structuring algorithms that are targeted at the problems found in wireless sensor networks. We discuss necessary and beneficial properties of structures, the design space of structuring algorithms and the requirements for different application scenarios. Second, we present new algorithms for several problems covering the distinctive characteristics of sensor networks: cooperative sensing, communication and location awareness. The problems are energy-efficient routing, time-bounded and space-bounded sensing, range-free boundary recognition, and partitioning of the network. Although the algorithms solve different types of problems, they are similar regarding the difficulties they are dealing with: unstable communication links, node failures and missing knowledge about the network topology prior to deployment. At the same time, a certain level of quality of service regarding network functionality and a predictable network lifetime are required.

Our work on the problem of energy-efficient routing structures led to the routing metric GEM^x (Gain per Energy Maximization) which considers both transport reliability and energy consumption. This metric is tunable and can adapt to changing environments providing for transport reliability while optimizing the energy consumption if possible. Moreover, it includes other

Abstract

energy-efficient routing metrics as special cases and provides an efficient solution for three popular link-layer acknowledgment models: explicit, implicit and lazy acknowledgment schemes. This approach behaves better than existing routing metrics currently used for routing in wireless sensor networks. Moreover, this new adaptive routing metric allows for a profound theoretical analysis of the family of energy-efficient routing metrics and the generated energy-efficient tree structure.

The detection of complex events, e.g., a fire, requires the analysis of a combination of several physical characteristics. Since it it often impractical and energy-inefficient to equip one sensor node with all required sensors, the cooperation of multiple nodes is required. Our work on space-bounded and time-bounded sensing is targeted at these scenarios with heterogeneous sensor networks in which different sensors are attached to one or several sensor nodes. We propose a set of algorithms called *ST-Grouping* for structuring the network by grouping sensor nodes in each other's vicinity to form groups possessing all required sensors. These groups act together as logical sensor nodes that are able to detect a complex event by cooperative sensing. Additionally, our solution allows scheduling the required sensing tasks within a group to meet timing dependencies between different physical sensors.

In many wireless sensor network scenarios, the random deployment of hundreds of sensor nodes without localization hardware raises the problem of determining the topology of the network in terms of the outer boundary and the boundaries of communication holes. Existing boundary recognition algorithms are able to determine these boundaries with certain guarantees. However, they only work for extremely dense networks and involve high computational and message complexities. In the context of this research, we propose an alternative and more general approach which works well for both sparse and dense topologies. Additionally, each node can calculate its guaranteed minimum distance to the network boundary. The proposed algorithm is also parameterized and can be adapted to the node density in the region.

Location-aware query processing in multi-sink scenarios poses additional challenges compared to plain wireless sensor networks, for example, the partitioning of the nodes between different sinks, the cooperation of these sinks and the coordination of their interactions with the wireless sensor network. The scenario that motivates our research of this topic stems from the "AWARE" research project. The role of multiple sinks interacting with a wireless sensor network might be fulfilled by preinstalled laptops, PDAs carried by people or unmanned aerial vehicles (UAVs). The proposed solution to this problem involves a hierarchical grouping of sensor nodes into *Convex*

Groups. This is a powerful abstraction for partitioning the wireless network among multiple sinks while ensuring their efficient cooperation for location-aware query processing. Moreover, convex groups provide support for the mobility of multiple sinks which is essential for rescue scenarios involving UAVs such as "AWARE".

Finally, based on the experience gained from development of structuring algorithms for sensor networks, we derived properties of the structuring algorithms and corresponding structures that are applicable to different kinds of scenarios.

Abstract

1 Introduction

This chapter introduces the topic of this thesis. We start with the motivation underlying this work, then list the major contributions provided and give an overview of the rest of this thesis.

1.1 Motivation

The field of wireless sensor networks has undergone a rapid evolution in the last years. The concept of having large networks of small-scale, spatially distributed, autonomous devices that use sensors and wireless communication for cooperatively monitoring their environment has inspired a variety of research activities and has also started to be used in real-world applications.

A single sensor node is very limited in its resources and capabilities and is nothing more than an isolated sensing device. The true power of wireless sensor networks lies in the large number of nodes cooperating in fulfilling a collective sensing task. However, such cooperation requires that the nodes are organized in a meaningful structure. Examples of such structuring of the network include partitioning of the network into clusters, assignment of roles to individual nodes and creation of trees for routing and aggregation purposes.

In large-scale wireless sensor networks distributed over a sizable area, it is impossible to either preplan structures in all detail prior to deployment or to generate and maintain structures manually. On the one hand, these problems are due to the size of the network and the complexity of the inter-node dependencies. On the other hand, the inherent dynamics of wireless networks (e.g., continuously changing connectivity graphs or possibly temporary failures of nodes) require the ability to adapt structures to changing realities at any time. Consequently, sensor nodes must be able to organize themselves autonomously.

Generating meaningful structures that effectively support distributed applications in the network is one of the major challenges in wireless sensor networks. Many research initiatives have tackled individual structuring problems such as finding an optimal routing tree structure.

One of the main goals of the work presented in this thesis is to provide a better understanding of structures in wireless sensor networks and their influence on the performance of applications running in wireless sensor networks. For this reason, we build four different structuring algorithms and investigate their properties and the properties of the resulting structures.

1.2 Contribution

This thesis provides several contributions to the field of wireless sensor networks in general and to the area of structures and structuring in wireless sensor networks in particular.

We thoroughly discuss the concept of structures and structuring algorithms in wireless sensor networks. While structures have always played an important role in sensor networks, a discussion of their fundamental properties has been missing so far. We identify different types of structures, classify both structures and structuring algorithms and derive important requirements for an effective and efficient structuring of wireless sensor networks.

We investigate three representative wireless sensor network applications for identifying particularly common and important types of structures used in wireless sensor networks. For four of these types of structures we introduce novel solutions that improve significantly upon the state of the art in their respective fields.

The first structuring approach that we discuss in this thesis provides a novel routing metric GEM^x that can be used to generate efficient routing tree structures with a special emphasis on energy efficiency in wireless sensor networks. Our first contribution in this context is the construction of a realistic model of the various influences on energy efficiency. The routing metric GEM^x is constructed based on this model. This metric takes into account both the expected gain and the expected energy consumption of paths. What sets GEM^x apart from other routing metrics is the fact that it is tunable to the conflicting goals of energy efficiency and transport reliability. This provides for a high degree of flexibility in creating the structure for routing data to the sink node of a wireless sensor network. Moreover, other routing metrics are included as special cases of GEM^x. Another distinguishing feature of GEM^x is that it considers the link layer acknowledgment scheme used thereby avoiding conflicts between the optimization goals of the two layers.

Our second structuring approach, *ST-Grouping*, deals with the formation of groups of nodes in the network. The motivating application for these groups is the detection of complex events by means of multiple nodes cooperating and complementing each other's set of sensors. Two algorithms for the formation of such spatial groups are presented: a greedy approach and an approach based on backtracking. In addition to performing this grouping, *ST-Grouping* also deals with scheduling the individual sensing tasks on the nodes forming a group.

Besides structures that can be generated and maintained in the network with the help of a structuring algorithm, there are also certain types of structures that already exist in any sensor network but need to be extracted prior to their use by the application. One important example is the boundary of a sensor network, which our third structuring approach deals with. Our first contribution in this field is to provide a clear definition of the boundary of a network and network holes with and without positions. This includes the formulation of several fundamental limits of solutions provided by any past or future approach. The second contribution is a boundary recognition algorithm that does not require any location information and works based on purely local neighborhood knowledge thus ensuring the scalability of the approach. The behavior of the algorithm can be flexibly controlled with the help of parameters. We show in the evaluation that our boundary recognition algorithm is able to work with significantly lower node densities than other existing approaches.

Finally, our fourth structuring algorithm deals with the problem of partitioning the nodes of a wireless sensor network among multiple sink nodes. The goal is to provide for efficient spatial queries in a network with multiple sinks collecting data from sensor nodes when both sink nodes and sensor nodes can experience limited mobility. Our approach, *Convex Groups*, uses knowledge on the geographic coordinates of the nodes to partition the application area and the nodes located within this area among the individual sink nodes thereby defining their respective areas of responsibilities. The efficiency of the *Convex Groups* approach is provided by conducting the partitioning in a hierarchical manner along the routing tree from the sensor nodes to the sink node. This allows to minimize the message overhead of distributing spatial queries.

The major contributions of this thesis have been published in important international scientific conferences, namely EWSN 2006 [SML+06], IPSN 2008 [SSG+08] and DCOSS 2008 [SSM08]. Extended versions of the first two papers are currently under review for a journal publication. Results of this research were applied in two systems developed within the Sustainable Bridges project [BRI] and the Aware project [AWA] and form a part of the TinyCubus framework [MMLR05b, MMLR05a, MLM⁺04] by providing tunable algorithms for structuring wireless sensor networks. Additional auxiliary work on structuring algorithms not discussed in this thesis has been presented at REALWSN 2008 [SSMM08] and SECON 2008 [GSH⁺08].

1.3 Structure

The rest of this thesis is structured as follows. The following chapter provides in depth introduction to wireless sensor networks and explains the importance of structures and structuring algorithms in this context. It provides a classification of structures and discusses fundamental requirements for different types of structuring algorithms. With the help of three representative applications, we identify particularly important types of structures which are then elaborated on in the following chapters.

In Chapters 3 to 6, we introduce our four individual structuring approaches. Chapter 3 discusses the routing metric GEM^x. In Chapter 4, we describe the *ST-Grouping* approach for dynamically forming groups for cooperative sensing. Next, our boundary recognition approach is presented in Chapter 5. We discuss the partitioning of nodes with *Convex Groups* in Chapter 6. For all four structuring approaches, we provide thorough discussions of their properties, evaluation and comparison to their respective related work.

Finally, we summarize the contributions of this thesis in Chapter 7 reflecting on the concept of structures based on the insights provided by the four specific representatives discussed before. We also discuss several possible extensions of our approaches and give a more general outlook on future research directions.

2 Structures in Wireless Sensor Networks

This chapter provides an overview of wireless sensor networks at the node and network level, introduces the concept of structures that appear as a result of the cooperation among sensor nodes and describes important network properties. We classify structures often found in sensor networks and motivate the need for an analysis of structuring algorithms. Based on the overview of various algorithms for sensor networks and their application areas, we extract requirements for structuring algorithms that lead to the formation of good quality structures.

2.1 Wireless Sensor Networks

Within the last ten years, the field of wireless sensor networks received significant attention by researchers. This section provides a short summary of the state of the art properties of sensor network platforms at both the node and the network level.

2.1.1 Sensor Nodes

A sensor node is a small device equipped with a microcontroller, flash memory, application specific sensors and a radio chip [HHKK04]. A number of prototypes and commercially available sensor nodes are on the market: Berkeley Motes (Mica, Mica2, MicaZ, Mica2dot) [XBO], Telos [PSC05], BTNode [BKM⁺04], UCLA iBadge [Sav02], Jennic [JEN], Sentilla Mini [SEN], etc.

While advances in processor speed and memory size generally follow Moore's Law, a substantial part of technological advances will be invested into the miniaturization of the devices. Since the progress in energy technology is much slower, *energy* remains the most limited resource of a wireless node. Energy consumption determines the *lifetime* of a sensor node and the sensor network as a whole. Wireless communication is the most expensive operation in terms of energy and, therefore, sensor network application components at all levels must aim at minimizing the amount of communication.

Due to resource constraints and the specific focus of sensor network applications, operating systems for sensor nodes are normally less complex and powerful than general-purpose operating systems. TinyOS [tin] is the de facto standard operating system specifically designed for wireless sensor nodes. It is based on an event-driven programming model. TinyOS itself and the application level programs are written in NesC – a programming language specifically designed for event-based embedded systems.

Some other popular sensor network operating systems are Contiki [DGV04], SOS [HCM05] and MANTIS [BCD$^+$05]. Contiki and SOS are also event-driven systems like TinyOS. Additionally, Contiki provides a thread-like programming abstraction with small memory overhead on top of the event-based core. SOS is known for its support of loadable modules and dynamic memory management. Unlike event-driven systems, MANTIS is based on preemptive multithreading by dividing the time between active processes and deciding which process can be currently run.

High heterogeneity of hardware and software platforms for sensor networks is a result of numerous attempts to customize the functionality of individual sensor nodes for a specific scenario. Algorithms proposed in this thesis have been implemented for TinyOS on the TelosB platform and have been tested in real world experiments. However, the developed concepts do not rely on any specific hardware or software platform.

Individual sensor nodes are usually of low value and interest. Instead, the power of sensor networks lies in the fact that a large number of small and cheap nodes can be organized in networks that cover an extended geographical area and cooperate in gathering information on the state of the real world.

2.1.2 Sensor Networks

In wireless sensor networks, spatially distributed sensor nodes communicate in an ad-hoc manner in which links and routes among nodes are formed and adjusted dynamically. The nodes also cooperatively monitor the state of the environment. On the one hand, sensor networks have much in common with traditional wired and wireless networks and, therefore, many existing approaches from these fields have been adapted to sensor networks. On the other hand, the importance of the *spatial distribution* of sensor nodes, their *ad-hoc communication* and their *sensing capabilities* constitute the main differences of wireless sensor networks from traditional wired networks. Compared to ad-hoc networks, sensor networks have much stronger resource constraints and less access to external infrastructure.

In traditional wired networks, the geographic locations of nodes rarely play an important role in ensuring the proper network functionality. However, for the deployment of a sensor network, the spatial distribution of sensor nodes within the area of interest is very important. Coverage detection, hole detection, topology control and boundary recognition algorithms can only be applied once the sensor network has been deployed.

Sensor networks belong to the class of ad-hoc networks due to their use of wireless ad-hoc communication that allows the sensor nodes to communicate directly with each other, possibly over multihop paths, without the need for a fixed infrastructure. This distinguishing feature provides for a wide applicability of sensor networks.

Finally, sensor nodes are equipped with sensors that monitor the state of the environment. This context data is used by more powerful devices for further analysis and permanent storage.

The exceptional properties of wireless sensor networks come from the combination of networking and sensing at different locations. The complexity of communication and cooperative sensing among the large set of nodes is difficult to manage from the outside. Instead, it is important that the nodes are able to organize themselves autonomously. If such self-organization works efficiently and effectively, useful patterns arise from relatively simple interactions among the nodes. In this thesis we refer to these patterns as *structures*.

A sensor network can be thought of as a graph in which nodes are mapped to vertices and wireless links are mapped to edges. Many distributed algorithms rely on a graph representation of the sensor network. Such algorithms tend to structure the sensor network in a graph-oriented way by organizing sensor nodes in canonical subgraph structures: trees and groups.

Another crucial aspect of sensor networks is geometry. Geometry comes into play because geometric constraints are usually imposed on the distribution of nodes over the space and the propagation range of wireless links. Therefore, in this thesis we concentrate on sensor network structures that originate from graph theory or geometry.

The next section describes structures that are frequently found in sensor networks and classifies their properties independent of the algorithms that accomplish such structuring of the network.

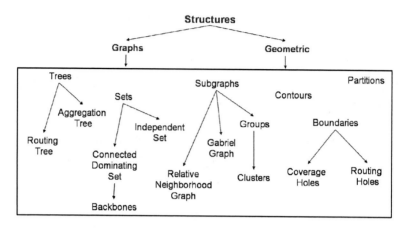

Figure 2.1: Classification of structures

2.2 Structures

Wendy Pullan defines structure as follows [Pul00]: "A structure is a fundamental but sometimes intangible concept covering the recognition, observation, nature, and stability of patterns and relationships of entities.". We define the *structure of a sensor network* as a relationship between individual sensor nodes. Structures often result from self-organization of the sensor nodes to form a sensor network. Bringing structure to a network is a goal of many network-level algorithms for sensor networks.

Routing and aggregation trees, clustering and hierarchical groupings of nodes, partitioning of sensor networks among multiple sinks, backbones and hole boundaries are all examples of common structures in wireless sensor networks. See Fig. 2.1 for an overview of the most popular examples.

At different levels of abstraction, structures can be seen as roles or overlays. At the node level, every node has a certain *role* with respect to other nodes in the sensor network. Examples of such roles are "aggregator", "cluster head", "parent", "child", etc. From the network perspective, any structure can be seen as an *overlay* over the sensor network.

Based on the nature of the structure, we differentiate between global and local structures. *Local structures* depend on the topology of a limited part of the network, and change only if the topology of this part changes. Examples of such local structures are some types of groupings or clusterings of nodes, the network boundary and boundaries of routing or coverage holes, some topology control structures. *Global structures* depend on the topology of the whole network. Examples are tree structures, multi-sink network partitioning, optimal aggregation and storage point placements, TDMA-based MAC protocols, etc. However, local structures are not always built using purely local knowledge. For example, many algorithms for the recognition of network boundaries operate on the whole network, e.g. [FK06b, KFPF06].

There are *flat* and *hierarchical* structures. Hierarchical structures are usually global structures and are an efficient and scalable way to reduce the complexity of the transition from individual nodes to a globally structured network.

As it has been discussed in Subsection 2.1.2, reasoning about sensor networks requires applying a combination of graph theory and geometry due to the importance of the spatial distribution of sensor nodes and ad-hoc communication between them. From this viewpoint, the structures in sensor networks can be classified based on their relation to these two fields of study. The notions of trees, backbones, connected dominating sets and independent sets are defined in a purely graph-theoretical way and, therefore, are classified in this thesis as *graph-based*. Area partitioning and boundaries of routing or coverage holes cannot be defined without considering the specifics of the sensor network deployment and are called *geometry-based*. Various clusters and node groupings can be graph-based or geometry-based depending on the goal of the node grouping.

Most structures in sensor networks are *constructed* as a result of collaboration among the sensor nodes, for example trees, groups, partitions. However, there are also structures that are already present in the network and that can be *extracted* with the help of appropriate algorithms. Examples of such geometry-based structures of a sensor network include the outer boundary and boundaries of holes which describe the topological shape of the network once it is deployed. The connectivity graph, the minimum connected dominating set and the maximum independent set are graph-based structures that can be extracted and provide additional information about the network deployment.

An overview of all listed properties of structures, independent of the structuring algorithm is given in Fig. 2.2.

In the following section, we describe several popular application areas of sensor networks with regard to the types of structures they require and extract specific requirements for the kinds of structures and their properties

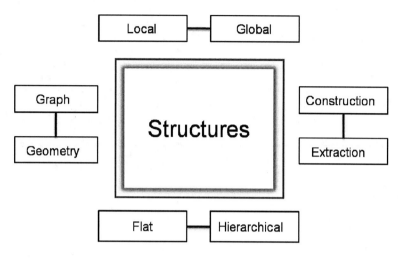

Figure 2.2: Properties of structures

which motivate the need for the research presented in this thesis.

2.3 Applications

There are a number of different application fields for sensor networks including environmental monitoring [LBV06], habitat monitoring [JOW+02], structural monitoring [MBFM07,MSKG05], smart environments [MMLR05c], health monitoring [MOJ06], disaster management [AWA], and tracking applications [ABC+03]. Due to resource constraints and application-dependent sensor hardware, there are many differences in software systems for each kind of application. However, there are also a number of similarities in the types of algorithms used and, consequently, the structures created.

Most static applications require some way of routing data to the data sink. This forces the sensor nodes to organize themselves in a routing tree (usually optimized for a specific goal, see Chapter 3 for examples). In lifetime-critical application scenarios, further optimization of communication can be achieved by aggregating sensor readings on the path to the sink which results in tree-based [JNRS06] or cluster-based structures [HCB00]. Another way of optimizing energy usage is realized by topology control algorithms that construct a backbone structure (a connected dominating set) for transporting

Figure 2.3: Nomotida: Monitoring of civil structures

data consisting of nodes with high energy [GZaDdA+05].

Application scenarios for mobile nodes often involve several sink nodes which poses network partitioning and node grouping problems. In general, sensor network systems that provide additional support for mobile applications avoid building sophisticated structures due to the overhead of structure maintenance. Therefore, local structures are mostly reasonable in this case.

We now discuss three different real-world systems for sensor networks and analyze the structures present in these systems. The author of this thesis was involved in the development or the testing and evaluation phase for each of these systems.

2.3.1 Nomotida

Nomotida [NOM] has been developed within the Sustainable Bridges EU Project [BRI] to provide the infrastructure and algorithms necessary for cost-effective monitoring of civil structures and detection of structural defects (for example on bridges as in Fig. 2.3). In conventional systems, sensors that measure physical parameters are connected to the data acquisition unit via cables. The installation of such a unit is costly, both in terms of time and money. The *Nomotida* system provides similar functionality but uses wireless communication and is simple, inexpensive and quick to install. It detects major structural changes or the failure of critical elements in a timely fashion and aims to improve the overall safety and reliability of civil structures. Additionally, monitoring provides valuable data for an end of life prediction. Elements exposed to fatigue can be kept under surveillance and, based on the acquired data, their remaining lifetime can be effectively estimated.

The *Nomotida* prototype has been tested on a number of steel bridges in Europe (Stork Bridge in Switzerland, Keraesjokk Bridge in Norway, Temmesjoki Bridge in Finland) and is currently being commercialized. The prototype installation consists of one sink node and several static sensor nodes deployed two years ago and still running on the Stork Bridge, Switzerland. The sensor nodes are equipped with accelerometers to measure natural vibrations of the cables of the bridge. They also possess temperature and humidity sensors. The sensor nodes have been mounted manually to the cables of the bridge and, therefore, form a regular structure.

The *Nomotida* system constructs and continuously maintains a routing tree structure. A many-to-one routing protocol based on the energy-efficient routing metric GEM [SML+06] described in Chapter 3 of this thesis is then used to build a routing path from any node in the network to the data sink.

In case of an event (e.g., a break in the construction) the sensor nodes form groups that have sensed the same event. This information is then routed to the base station.

The *Nomotida* system is a very good example of a static sensor network deployment for monitoring and data acquisition purposes. The main optimization characteristic of the *Nomotida* network is energy efficiency of the network due to high requirements on the system operation and, thus, network lifetime.

2.3.2 Aware

The *Aware* system is developed as part of the AWARE EU Project [AWA] and focuses on disaster management and civil security scenarios. The *Aware* network consists of a wireless sensor network with both static and mobile nodes, unmanned aerial vehicles (UAVs) and mobile devices carried by people which act as data sinks. In case of fire, sensor nodes are dynamically deployed by UAVs and start measuring environmental characteristics such as temperature, humidity and gas level. Every sensor node is equipped with a low-power GPS receiver. Based on the analysis of the video information

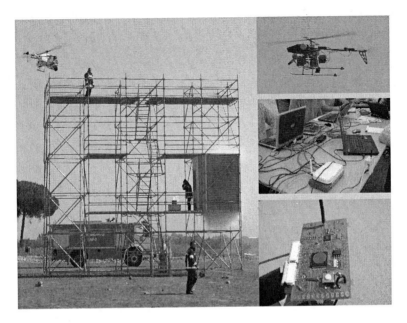

Figure 2.4: Aware: Support for disaster management

and the sensor readings, the mission coordinator can rate the scale and the spread of fire, and eventually the location of fire-fighters and fire-trucks.

The *Aware* prototype has been tested in Utrera, Spain (see images of experiments in Fig. 2.4) and is currently in its final year of development and testing.

A number of different structures are used in this scenario: A routing tree enables the transmission of sensor data to the nearest sink and a boundary recognition algorithm is used to detect holes in the network. The partitioning of the sensor network among multiple sink nodes improves the efficiency of accessing the sensor data and of disseminating location dependent queries. The on-demand grouping of sensor nodes as a reaction to a fire event and the subsequent aggregation of sensor readings within the group is used to increase the confidence in inferring the event.

The target system operation time is limited to one week. The main requirements for the *Aware* network are high reliability and robustness.

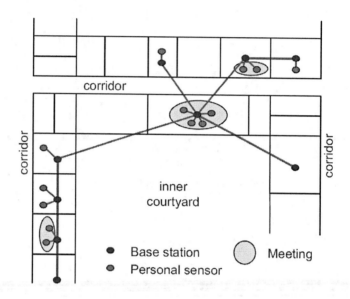

corridor

corridor

corridor

inner
courtyard

● Base station   ◯ Meeting
◉ Personal sensor

Figure 2.5: Sense-R-Us: Smart environments (taken from [MMLR05c])

2.3.3 Sense-R-Us

Sense-R-Us [MMLR05c] is an experimental application focused on building a Smart Environment using Mica2 sensor nodes. It was first deployed in the Computer Science Department at the University of Stuttgart for one week (see Fig. 2.5). The system records the movement and meeting patterns of employees in the deployed area in order to derive information about the duration and composition of meetings. Thereby, *Sense-R-Us* is able to provide statistics on the overall department performance and time distribution.

There are two types of sensor nodes used by *Sense-R-Us*: location-aware static base station nodes installed in all office rooms and personal sensors carried by employees. The base stations periodically send beacon messages that include their location information. Personal sensors determine their current positions by selecting the base station they can hear with the highest signal strength. They also send beacons which are used by other personal sensors to update their respective neighborhood lists. These lists together

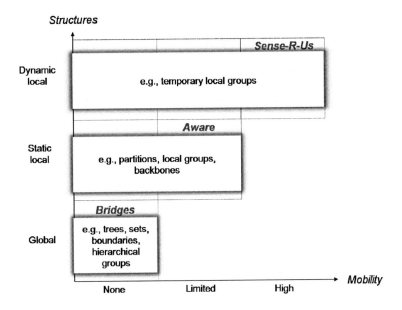

Figure 2.6: Classification of example systems and their requirements on structures

with microphone data are used to detect the occurrence of meetings.

As follows from the description above, the *Sense-R-Us* network assumes an indoor installation and includes both static and mobile nodes. The system periodically runs a meeting detection algorithm and stores the result in flash. The only structure constructed by the *Sense-R-Us* system is a temporary node grouping based on neighborhood relationship between personal nodes and recorded microphone activities.

2.3.4 Similarities of Structures

The three presented sensor network systems cover a large portion of the sensor network design space: indoor and outdoor, static and mobile networks, regular and random deployments.

Structures can be found in each of the presented system. The systems developed for static scenarios, e.g., Nomotida, tend to construct global structures like a routing tree to transfer the data from the sensor nodes to one or several base stations. Building local (often temporary) groups is popular among the systems that have to support node mobility, which is the case for *Aware* and *Sense-R-Us*. Local groups incur a relatively small construction overhead and generally simplify operations inside of the group due to the limited number of group members, a simplified topology and the local nature of the group. Fig. 2.6 summarizes relevant properties of structures built by the discussed systems. Additionally, we classify the structures with respect to their support for node mobility.

Trees, subgraphs and sets are often used in sensor network algorithms dealing with the cooperation among sensor nodes. This is due to the fact that graph information is available in all networks and does not require sophisticated knowledge of network properties and system application specifics. However, knowledge of node coordinates, as in the *Aware* network, allows to benefit from building more sophisticated geometry-oriented structures. For example, a partitioning of the wireless network among multiple sinks can be used to improve the efficiency of the location-based query dissemination.

In the next section we give an overview of the requirements on and the properties of algorithms for sensor networks that construct and extract different kinds of structures.

2.4 Structuring Algorithms

In many cases, distributed algorithms define a relationship between the elements of the network and thus determine the structure of sensor networks. While a structure is often assumed to be stable over time, one has to account for considerable dynamics of sensor networks. Main sources of these dynamics include unstable communication links, node failures and constantly evolving environments.

There are plenty of publications focusing on finding optimal structures for wireless sensor networks. For example, the approaches described in [WTC03, QC06,SML+06] focus on the construction of an energy-efficient routing tree. In [JNRS06], the authors investigate the problem of constructing an optimal (with respect to the aggregation cost) aggregation tree. The clustering approach presented in [HCB00] balances the energy consumption in the network and, thus, prolongs the network lifetime. The boundary extraction algorithms described in [KFPF06,SSG+08] try to both minimize the uncertainty region of the boundary and extract boundaries for sparse networks.

The goals of sensor networks are achieved through cooperation of tens to thousands of sensor nodes. This requires high *scalability* of the distributed algorithms for sensor networks. Approaches that incorporate structures are more scalable than structure-free ones. Forming hierarchies as a way of structuring a network is the most widely used approach to increase algorithm scalability with the number of network entities. For example, the Internet could not scale to support today's number of Internet leaf networks without using hierarchies in its algorithms (e.g., in DNS or as part of routing). This underlines the importance of the development of algorithms for structuring sensor networks.

Several studies on the requirements for sensor network algorithms [KW05, RM04a] have confirmed the importance of the *QoS level*, the *energy efficiency* and the *scalability* aspects of such algorithms. These are general requirements for all algorithms in sensor networks, not only for those based on structuring.

Additionally, the last two requirements imply that the amount of communication should be limited and that algorithms should avoid depending on global knowledge about the network. This motivates that even global structures such as trees and hierarchical groups should be constructed using only *local neighborhood knowledge*.

From the perspective of time, the algorithms lead to the formation of either *dynamic (temporary)* or *static* structures. Temporary structures collapse after fulfilling their goal. For example, a grouping of nodes formed as the result of an event looses its meaning after passing a preprocessed event description to the base station. Static structures are maintained during the whole network lifetime.

If the application scenario allows for node mobility, the structures might change or break as soon as sensor nodes change their positions. Therefore, if a certain number of nodes in the network are mobile, the structuring algorithms should result in structures that do not degrade the network performance if unpredictable structure evolutions occur. For example, in *Sense-R-Us* [MMLR05c] and *ZebraNet* [JOW+02], only a local temporary grouping of neighboring sensor nodes is analyzed. Moreover, node mobility can cause *overhead* during structure update.

Static and global structures are not suitable for mobile scenarios even if the sensor nodes move with low speeds. This is because the transmission range of a wireless radio is quite short (normally from 30 to 100 meters). The major influencing factor is the share of mobile nodes. For this reason, the presence of several mobile nodes in the *Aware* network [AWA] makes it possible to

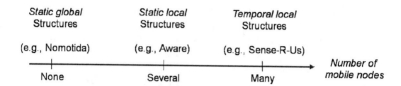

Figure 2.7: Classification of structures with respect to node mobility

construct and maintain network partitions efficiently with a relatively small update overhead.

In contrast, sensor network systems specifically developed for static scenarios can profit from using structures. Examples include Nomotida [NOM], TinyDB [MFHH05], the system described in [LBV06] and others. Fig. 2.7 summarizes this classification of structuring algorithms with respect to node mobility.

Even for static networks, node failures and the unstabile nature of wireless links can result in changes to the structures over time. Therefore, structuring algorithms should lead to the formation of *stable* and *reconfigurable* structures. Stable structures can deal with environmental influences up to a certain limit while avoiding the costs for repeated reconfigurations. A reconfiguration should be possible if significant changes of the environment happen, e.g., nodes fail or new nodes join the network. The algorithms must find a compromise between stability and reconfiguration properties of a structure based on the level of dynamics of the target environment. To account for this flexibility, structuring algorithms should additionally be *parameterized* and *adaptive*.

An algorithm that constructs a global structure over a sensor network usually requires a certain time to converge. *Convergence* is a precondition for reaching a stable structure. However, there are a number of algorithms that might oscillate in the general case, e.g., the role assignment algorithm described in [RFMB04]. The usage of these algorithms should be limited to cases for which they converge or eventually decide on a stable state.

The quality of a structure and, therefore, of the algorithm used for its construction or extraction depends on how good the underlying model approximates the target environment and how specific the model is. If the applied model badly reflects the specific properties of the target environment, the output of the structuring algorithm might degrade the network performance considerably. If the model used is too general, the algorithm can become

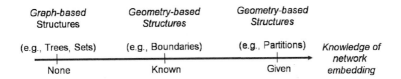

Figure 2.8: Classification of structures with respect to the knowledge of the network embedding

overly complicated resulting in a high overhead.

Further properties of the sensor network can be derived if knowledge of the network geometry is available. Since node localization is a NP-hard problem [AGY04] even with global knowledge and given distances between individual nodes, the extraction of geometry-based structures is quite difficult without further geometric information. From this perspective, we classify structuring algorithms in three groups. The first group of algorithms extract structures using only the graph representation of the sensor network. Such algorithms can result in *graph-based* structures only. The second group of algorithms rely on *some* knowledge about the embedding of the sensor network but do not require the knowledge of node coordinates. This knowledge includes one dimensional characteristics of the geographic locations of sensor nodes, such as distances between individual sensor nodes or specifics of the radio propagation model (UDG, d-QUDG). Examples of such algorithms include the boundary-recognition approaches described in [KFPF06, SSG$^+$08]. The last group of algorithms profits from the use of low-power, low-precision GPS receivers by all or some of the nodes in the network. We say that all algorithms that rely on geometry information of any kind result in *geometry-based* structures as depicted in Fig. 2.8.

Finally, a structure can be built by an algorithm in a *top-down* or *bottom-up* fashion depending on the properties of the structure. For example, divide and conquer-based approaches build structures in a top-down manner whereas greedy solutions start constructing a structure from the bottom.

Fig. 2.9 provides an overview of the requirements on algorithms with respect to structure. Note that we skip the general requirements on algorithms for sensor networks like QoS, use of local knowledge, and energy efficiency.

In the next section, we motivate the selection of the structuring algorithms presented in this thesis.

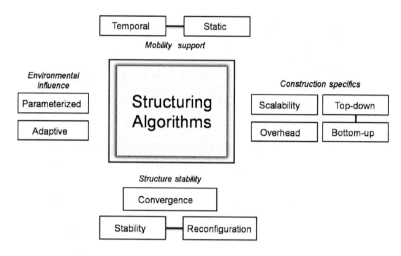

Figure 2.9: Design space of structuring algorithms

2.5 Selection

An analysis of different systems for sensor networks in Section 2.3 has shown the following structuring algorithms to be of particular importance: tree construction algorithms (e.g., routing, aggregation trees), group construction algorithms (e.g., clustering, node grouping) and topology extraction algorithms (e.g., network partitioning, coverage and connectivity extraction, network boundaries).

As part of this thesis we have developed four algorithms for structuring sensor networks that cover all of these types and generate widely used structures. They also cover the essential aspects of wireless sensor networks: sensing, communication and location awareness. These algorithms are:

Routing This algorithm solves the problem of constructing an energy-efficient *routing tree*. While analyzing the problem of routing tree construction, we reason about the main properties such a routing tree structure has to possess – consistency, optimality and loop-freeness – and their relation to energy efficiency as an optimization goal.

ST-Grouping This algorithm considers the problem of capturing complex events that are hard to record with a single sensor node. To deal with that, we perform a spatial and temporary non-hierarchical *node*

Properties of Structures	Routing	ST-Grouping	Boundary Recogn.	Convex Groups
Global/Local	G	L	L	G
Flat/Hierarchical	H	F	F	H
Graph/Geometry-based	Gr	Gr/Geo	Geo	Geo
Construction/Extraction	C	C	E	C/E

Table 2.1: Properties of structures resulted by developed algorithms

grouping and subsequently distribute the partial sensing tasks among the nodes in the group.

Boundary Recognition The extraction of network *boundaries* provides important knowledge on the topology of a sensor network. Our algorithm performs such an extraction without requiring node positions. Additionally we present a thorough analysis of the properties of the obtained structure.

Convex Groups This algorithm uses the knowledge of node coordinates to construct (or extract) an efficient *partitioning* of the sensor network among multiple sink nodes in a way that optimizes the querying of different parts of the network.

Every algorithm provides a solution for a separate problem and is by itself a valuable contribution to the field of wireless sensor networks. The *Routing* and the *Boundary Recognition* algorithms also include a profound analysis of the problem properties, provide solutions that are qualitatively better than existing ones and include a number of theoretical findings that, we believe, advance the understanding of these problems. The *ST-Grouping* and *Convex Groups* are simple and practical algorithms that provide an efficient solution for problems found in the *Nomotida* and *Aware* systems.

These structuring algorithms differ in the types of resulting structures. *Routing* and *ST-Grouping* belong to the group of structure *construction* algorithms whereas *Boundary Recognition extracts* topology information of the deployed network. The *Convex Groups* approach can be seen, on the one hand, as a *construction* algorithm that builds responsibility zones for every mobile sink node. On the other hand, *Convex Groups* hierarchically *extracts* the convex hull of each partition. The Partitioning itself is hidden in the underlying routing algorithm.

The groups built by *ST-Grouping* and the boundaries extracted by the *Boundary Recognition* algorithms are local structures in contrast to routing trees and partitions. *Convex Groups* is the only algorithm that uses

39

the knowledge of sensor node coordinates acquired with low-power GPS receivers. Boundaries and partitions are also geometry-based structures and rely on certain knowledge about the deployment (embedding) of the sensor network.

Table 2.1 summarizes the properties of the structures generated by the algorithms developed as a part of this thesis and shows that our selection covers a large spectrum of different combinations.

In the next chapters, we are going to present each algorithm in detail as well as discuss the problem description, its application areas and evaluate the solution performance. Moreover, based on the important properties of the structuring algorithms and their classification discussed in Section 2.4, we analyze each algorithm and derive important rules and insights about the structuring of sensor networks.

3 Routing

In this chapter, we tackle the core part of the routing layer – the *routing metric* – which is responsible for selecting the best path. Our goal is energy efficiency and, therefore, we first analyze energy efficiency with respect to routing metrics – a prerequisite ignored in prior work. We construct a realistic model of the influences on energy efficiency including different link layer acknowledgement schemes. Building on these insights, we propose the new routing metric GEM^x. We discuss limitations and weaknesses of existing energy efficient metrics and compare their performance with our approach. We also show that our new metric encompasses existing ones as special cases and dispute the simplifications and assumptions of previous metrics. Concerning the routing tree structure itself, we analyze routing metrics based on the consistency, optimality and loop-freeness properties the routing tree has to fulfil.

3.1 Preliminaries

Routing is one of the most critical tasks in any network and, therefore, a considerable amount of research has been conducted for traditional wired networks, cellular networks, ad-hoc networks with and without support for mobility and also wireless sensor networks. In the last years, a number of routing algorithms have been proposed for wireless sensor networks. These algorithms cover one-to-one [BE02], one-to-many [MFHH02,DCO04], many-to-one [IGE00, WTC03, BS07, GYHG04] and many-to-many [SY07] routing tasks. We focus on many-to-one routing since it reflects the predominant communication pattern [WTC03]. For many-to-one routing, a routing tree is typically built to allow transporting data from any node to a *base station*. However, many of the identified issues and proposed solutions of this chapter are not limited to routing trees but are applicable to network paths in general and, therefore, to the other routing paradigms as well.

The routing task can be split into several parts. We examine the *routing metric* which is used to choose between alternative available paths in order to select the best one, where "best" is evaluated based on a predefined optimization goal. The routing metric has the largest influence on the resulting routing tree and, thus, on the provided quality and cost of the communication in the network.

Although energy efficient routing is the focus of a number of research papers, a clear definition of *energy efficiency* with respect to routing is often missing or incomplete. We discuss the challenges and properties of energy efficiency as a goal for routing metrics. Additionally, we show that the model used by existing metrics is too simplistic. We then provide a model that reliably captures the characteristics influencing energy efficiency. This includes the modeling of the link layer, particularly the implemented acknowledgement scheme. Based on this model, we propose the new metric GEM^x that incorporates the rules necessary to build a routing tree optimized for energy efficiency. This metric is parameterized in order to allow putting the emphasis either on increasing transport reliability or on saving energy. Additionally, we show that existing metrics are special cases of this new metric and examine the differences in the underlying models. Based on the advanced model and the discussion of energy efficiency itself, we analyze our new metric and the existing metrics and discuss several important properties such as optimality and loop-freeness of the resulting routing tree and the influence of node parameters such as the maximum number of retransmissions. In our evaluation, we show the performance of different metrics and examine the strengths and weaknesses of each.

3.2 Background and Related Work

A huge number of routing metrics for traditional, ad-hoc and sensor networks exist with a variety of optimization goals and types of input values [BHSW07]. Optimization goals include the path length, the delay, the bandwidth, the throughput and many more. The input values are usually the corresponding link metrics like delay, bandwidth and throughput but can also include, for example, the load of a node on the path.

In wireless sensor networks, a significant part of the characteristics is the same for all nodes or links (e.g., delay, bandwidth). Additionally, a large number of path metrics do not play a critical role in typical scenarios including delay and throughput. We concentrate on energy efficient routing and, therefore, limit the network model to only represent relevant values such as the transport reliability of a link and the transmission power level of a node. These characteristics are the same or a superset of the characteristics used in other existing energy efficient routing metrics.

We consider the underlying acknowledgement mechanisms on the link layer. Different schemes and their influence on routing are discussed in Section 3.3. Therefore, each characteristic associated with sending a packet (e.g., the probability of success) is combined with the corresponding acknowledgement characteristic.

Since one-to-many routing (dissemination) from the sink to the network is usually executed by a very different class of algorithms that exploit the broadcast characteristic of the wireless medium, we only consider messages from the nodes in direction to the sink.

In the following, we define the network model used and the terminology required to reason about routing metrics before introducing existing metrics proposed for energy-efficient routing. The terminology is also summarized in a table in Section 3.10.

3.2.1 Network Model and Terminology

The sensor network is modeled as a *directed* graph $G(V, E)$, where V represents a set of *vertices* (*nodes*) and E a set of *edges* (*links*). One special node with no energy constraints – usually numbered with 0 – is called the *base station* node or the *sink* node.

Each directed link is associated with a pair of characteristics: First, the probability $p \in Pr$ that a packet sent from the source node of the link to the destination node is correctly received, and second, the probability q that an acknowledgement from the destination node is correctly received by the source node. This pair of characteristics defines the *link connectivity* or the *link quality*. A link only exists if both probabilities are greater than 0. Therefore, $p, q \in (0, 1]$ holds if no blacklisting is used. Usually, the existence of a link $\langle u, v \rangle$ between two nodes $u, v \in V$ implies the existence of a reverse link. However, the characteristics of a link and its reverse link are not necessarily the same. Therefore, we consider asymmetrical links.

Each node spends energy for sending packets and for acknowledging received ones. These energy costs e_f and e_b are associated with each node in the graph. Note that e_f and e_b are elementary costs of sending or acknowledging exactly one packet respectively and do not take retransmissions into account. We consider the energy costs as being dimensionless entities: $e_f, e_b \in \mathbb{R}^+$. The values e_f and e_b are considered to be independent. However, it is also possible to define a relationship and express one value in terms of the other. In [QC06] the authors argue that e_b is considerably smaller than e_f

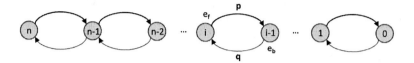

Figure 3.1: Path model of a path consisting of n nodes and a sink 0

and, therefore, assume the ratio $\lambda = \frac{e_b}{e_f}$ of both energy consumptions being constant in order to evaluate the per bit characteristics.

Both values e_f and e_b depend on the node's transmission power level l used for communication. For that reason, we assume the existence of a discrete function $e : \mathbb{L} \rightarrow \mathbb{R}^+ \times \mathbb{R}^+$, where $\mathbb{L} \in 2^{\mathbb{N}}$ is the set of available power levels. This function expresses the dependency between the transmission power level l and the pair of energiy costs $(e_f(l), e_b(l))$ required for transmitting a message and its acknowledgement.

Each node $i \in V$ initially possesses the amount of energy E^i_{init}. We assume that the *transmission power level* (TPL) l can be changed during the lifetime of a node based on the amount of energy left, based on different packet priorities or based on any other factor. Communication with higher transmission power levels might also increase the link quality p and thereby increase the probability of a successful packet delivery.

Besides using different TPLs, the nodes might also apply *retransmissions* of lost packets to increase the link quality between two nodes. The maximum number of retransmissions is always limited for a packet. However, this number can also be changed during the lifetime of a sensor node.

When considering a path d, we number the nodes on the path starting with n down to 0 from the packet source to the destination (cf. Fig. 3.1). We call this direction *upstream* and the reverse direction *downstream*. The link probabilities numbered along the path with p_i and q_i are the probabilities for successfully sending a packet or an acknowledgement respectively on the link from node i to node $i - 1$. Additionally, the energy costs are associated with the links where e_{f_i} equals e_f of node i and e_{b_i} equals e_b of node $i - 1$, since node $i - 1$ is responsible for sending the acknowledgement.

We define a routing tree T_G of the sensor network G as a tree rooted at the sink node where a simple path exists from any vertex $v \in V(T_G)$ to the sink. We only consider spanning trees of the strongly connected component of G that contains the sink. There usually exist a large number of such trees for a given graph. In this chapter, we consider the problem of many-to-one routing in wireless sensor networks: The goal is to find a tree T_G^{opt} which is optimal for a given G and some optimality criterion. In particular, we focus on energy-efficiency as the optimization goal.

In order to build the routing tree, a routing protocol uses a *routing metric* to choose between alternative paths in order to select the best based on a predefined optimization goal. The metric defines a partial order over all paths. However, as we will show later, the selection of the best path does not necessarily result in an optimal tree.

3.2.2 Algebra and Properties of Routing Metrics

The modeling of a routing metric as an algebra is used in [Sob05, YW08] to mathematically prove the following desirable properties of the routing trees generated by a metric: *consistency*, *optimality* and *loop-freeness*.

Assume a node n decides to route packets to the sink node 0 along the path d. This path is *consistent* if the subpath from any intermediate node A to the sink is the same as the path chosen by A (independently) for its own packets. The routing metric is *consistent* if all paths in a constructed routing tree are consistent.

The routing metric is *optimal* if all nodes in a constructed routing tree route packets along optimal paths. Here, optimality is defined by the routing metric itself (e.g., the shortest possible path). The routing metric is *loop-free* if its result is a correct tree and does not contain any cycles.

In order to prove these properties, the author of [Sob05] represents a routing metric as an algebra. The algebra is defined as a septet $(W, \preceq, L, \Sigma, \phi, \oplus, f)$ where L is a set of labels (corresponding to links), Σ is a set of signatures and $\oplus$ maps pairs of a label and a signature to a signature (corresponding to a path append operation). The special signature ϕ indicates the absence of a path. W is a set of weights and the function f maps from a signature to a weight. Finally, the relation $\preceq$ provides a total order of weights, where "lighter" values indicate preferred paths. Additionally, an algebra for routing must fulfill the following two intuitive conditions: $\forall l \in L, l \oplus \phi = \phi$ (a link appended to a non-existing path results in a non-existing path) and $\forall \alpha \in \Sigma \setminus \{\phi\}, f(\alpha) \prec f(\phi)$ (the weight of the non-existing path is maximal). To reason about the properties of a metric, the additional properties *isotonicity* and *monotonicity* of the algebra are used.

The algebra of a routing metric is *left-isotonic* if $f(\alpha) \preceq f(\beta)$ implies $f(l \oplus$

$\alpha) \preceq f(l \oplus \beta), \forall \alpha, \beta \in \Sigma$ and $l \in L$. Similarly, the algebra is *strictly left-isotonic* if $f(\alpha) \prec f(\beta)$ implies $f(l \oplus \alpha) \prec f(l \oplus \beta), \forall \alpha, \beta \in \Sigma$ and $l \in L$. Isotonicity expresses that if a path d_1 is better than a path d_2, then for every path consisting of a common prefix subpath d_p and d_1 and d_2 respectively, the path including d_1 is better.

The algebra is *left-monotonic* if $f(\alpha) \preceq f(b \oplus \alpha), \forall \alpha, \beta \in \Sigma$ and *strictly left-monotonic* if $f(\alpha) \prec f(\beta \oplus \alpha), \forall \alpha, \beta \in \Sigma \setminus \{\phi\}$. Monotonicity expresses that a path d is always better than the path d prefixed with some other path.

The authors of [YW08] show that for hop-by-hop routing based on the distributed Bellman-Ford algorithm the routing metric must be left-monotonic in order to be loop-free. The same is true for consistency. Additionally, they have proven that the combination of left-isotonicity and left-monotonicity guarantees optimality of a routing metric.

As we will discuss in Section 3.6.1, left-monotonicity is not sufficient to guarantee loop-freeness after a change in the underlying topology: Although the first constructed tree is guaranteed to be loop-free, repairs to the tree after changes in the topology can result in loops. For that reason, we require *strict* left-monotonicity to guarantee loop-freeness also in the case of topology changes. Additionally, strict left-monotonicity is also required for consistency and optimality if considering topology changes.

3.2.3 Existing Energy-Aware Routing Metrics

This section introduces the most popular group of existing routing metrics for sensor networks that optimize transport reliability and energy consumption of the paths in the routing tree. As shown in [CACM03], the *Shortest Path First* routing metric used in traditional networks performs badly when applied to sensor networks due to its tendency to select short but low quality and unstable paths to the sink. Therefore, a number of other routing metrics have been analyzed or developed specifically for sensor networks: *Shortest Path First with Blacklisting*, *Success Rate*, *Expected Transmission Count* and *Energy Per Bit*. In the following paragraphs we present the definitions and underlying ideas of these metrics.

Shortest Path First
The *Shortest Path First (SPF)* metric discussed in [WTC03, CACM03] se-

lects the route based only on the length of the path.

$$\text{SPF} = \sum_{i=1}^{n} 1 \rightarrow \mathbf{min} \tag{3.1}$$

In [CACM03], *SPF* has been shown to be unsuitable for sensor networks, because it tends to select the neighbor furthest away with the lowest link quality to route packets, as it is aiming to cover as much distance in direction of the destination in one step as possible.

Shortest Path First with Blacklisting
An enhanced version of *SPF*, called *Shortest Path First with Blacklisting* (*SPF(t)*) [WTC03], applies a blacklisting procedure to exclude links with a quality less than t before using the *SPF* algorithm on the resulting topology.

$$\text{SPF(t)} = \sum_{i=1}^{n} \| p_i q_{i-1} \|_h \rightarrow \mathbf{min}$$
$$\| p_i q_{i-1} \|_h = \begin{cases} 1, p_i q_{i-1} \geq t \\ \infty, p_i q_{i-1} < t \end{cases} \tag{3.2}$$

where $p_i q_{i-1}$ is the quality of the link between nodes i and $i-1$. On the one hand, *SPF(t)* clearly shows a better behavior than *SPF*. However, on the other hand, the use of blacklisting can lead to a disconnected routing tree [CACM03]. Moreover, both *SPF* and *SPF(t)* are only indirectly aware of link qualities and energy costs.

Success Rate
The *Success Rate* metric selects the path from node i to the sink with the highest end-to-end success rate. In [GYHG04], the authors discussed two possibilities to calculate the *SR* metric: As the product of the link reliabilities p_i along the path d (called *SR* in this thesis) or as the product of the forward and backward link reliabilities p_i and q_{i-1} along the path d (called *SRQ* in this thesis):

$$\text{SR} = \prod_{i=1}^{n} p_i \rightarrow \mathbf{max} \tag{3.3}$$

$$\text{SRQ} = \prod_{i=1}^{n} p_i q_{i-1} \rightarrow \mathbf{max} \tag{3.4}$$

The *SR* and *SRQ* metrics usually underestimate the path qualities, because neither takes the possibility of packet retransmissions into account and *SRQ*'s estimation of the path quality is too pessimistic due to the inclusion of the probability of receiving an acknowledgement. Both metrics can also lead to cycles in the routing graph if the link quality estimator allows links with 100% quality. Moreover, as shown in [SML$^+$06], the metrics are very unstable. Additionally, *SR* and *SRQ* are not energy-aware.

Expected Transmission Count
The *Expected Transmission Count (ETX)* [WTC03] metric was originally developed for ad-hoc networks but is used in sensor networks as well. Its goal is to minimize the sum of the expected number of transmissions along a path:

$$\text{ETX} = \sum_{i=1}^{n} \frac{1}{p_i q_{i-1}} \to \textbf{min} \tag{3.5}$$

ETX considers both the link quality and the energy consumption of a path. However, as we will show later, *ETX* assumes that a message is always successfully delivered which implies that the number of possible transmissions is unlimited. Therefore, *ETX* is not realistic and can be improved by limiting the maximum number of transmissions. Additionally, *ETX* does not take into account that nodes sending with different signal strengths consume different amounts of energy.

Energy Per Bit
In [QC06] the stream routing metric *Energy Per Bit (EPB)* was proposed for the stream path model which uses lazy link layer acknowledgements, which are discussed in Section 3.3:

$$\text{EPB} = \sum_{i=1}^{n} \frac{1}{p_i} + \frac{1-p_i}{p_i q_{i-1}} \lambda \to \textbf{min} \tag{3.6}$$

Remember that we defined λ as $\frac{e_b}{e_f}$. *EPB* sets the energy consumption of the path in relation to its quality. The authors showed that this metric significantly improves the routing layer efficiency. Similarly to *ETX*, this metric also fails to consider that the number of retransmissions is limited.

3.3 The Model

In this section we model the path characteristics: transport reliability and energy consumption. The model covers link and path layers presented separately in the following subsections.

3.3.1 Link Layer Acknowledgement Schemes

In this subsection we examine the three most popular acknowledgement schemes: explicit acknowledgements, implicit acknowledgements and lazy acknowledgements. We discuss each scheme separately and model the expected values for the *transport reliability* and the *energy consumption* of the link with respect to the underlying acknowledgement model used. The omission of acknowledgements altogether is not modeled separately since it corresponds to the special case of the implicit acknowledgement scheme when only one transmission is allowed.

Explicit Acknowledgements

Explicit acknowledgements are the most commonly used form of link layer acknowledgements. They are an attractive approach for low quality wireless links.

After node i sends a packet to node $i - 1$ (along the path), node i waits a predefined timeout period expecting node $i - 1$ to send an acknowledgement. If no acknowledgement is received – because either the packet or the acknowledgement is lost – the sender retransmits the packet.

Assume node i has to transmit a packet to node $i - 1$ using the explicit acknowledgements scheme. Let p be the probability of successful packet delivery over the directed link $\langle i, i-1 \rangle$ and let q be the probability of successful acknowledgement delivery in the reverse direction $\langle i-1, i \rangle$. Let e_f and e_b be the amount of energy spent for packet and acknowledgement transmission by nodes i and $i - 1$ respectively. Additionally, in case of a transmission failure, the nodes might retransmit the lost packet $r_p - 1$ times meaning that every packet is transmitted at most r_f times along the same link.

Below, we consider the following three cases: First, no retransmissions are possible. Second, the number of retransmissions is limited to some finite value, and third, the maximum number of retransmissions approaches infinity.

Case 1: No retransmissions ($r_f = 1$)

If no retransmissions of lost packets are allowed, the transport reliability of the forward link $R_{r_f}^{link}$ corresponds to the probability of a successful packet transmission by node i over the forward link $\langle i, i - 1 \rangle$.

$$R_{r_f}^{link} = p \tag{3.7}$$

We also model the energy consumption of the link $E_{r_f}^{link}$. Node i consumes e_f energy units for sending a packet along the forward link $\langle i, i - 1 \rangle$. This packet is successfully received at node $i - 1$ with the probability p. In this case, node $i - 1$ sends an explicit acknowledgement over the reverse link $\langle i - 1, i \rangle$. This consumes an additional amount of e_b energy units.

$$E_{r_f}^{link} = e_f + p e_b \tag{3.8}$$

There are two reasons for sending an explicit acknowledgement even when no retransmissions are allowed: First, the receiver does not necessarily know the maximum number of retransmissions of the sender as we consider this to be a node specific parameter that may even change over time, for example to adapt the behavior based on the remaining amount of energy of the node. Second, even if no retransmissions are allowed, sending an explicit acknowledgement can be used for notifying the sender node i about the successful transmission of the packet which helps in estimating the link quality. However, if the acknowledgement (and not the packet itself) is lost, this results in an underestimate of the transport reliability.

Case 2: Limited number of transmissions ($r_f \ll \infty$)

For this case let us assume that the number of transmission attempts at node i is limited to r_f. The transport reliability of the forward link in this case is improved by $p(1 - p)^{k-1}$ with every additional (the k-th) available transmission. Therefore, we have:

$$R_{r_f}^{link} = \sum_{k=1}^{r_f} p(1 - p)^{k-1} = 1 - (1 - p)^{r_f} \tag{3.9}$$

For the energy consumption of the link if a finite number of retransmissions is available, we consider the following: The cost of one attempt is $(e_f + p e_b)$

(c.f., above) and the probability that the packet is considered lost (due to packet loss or loss of the acknowledgement) exactly k times is $(1 - pq)^k$. Therefore, the expected value of the energy consumption is the sum from 0 to $r_f - 1$ of the product of these values.

$$E_{r_f}^{link} = \sum_{k=0}^{r_f-1} (1 - pq)^k (e_f + pe_b) = (e_f + pe_b) \frac{1 - (1 - pq)^{r_f}}{pq} \qquad (3.10)$$

Case 3: Infinite number of transmissions $(r_f \to \infty)$

Finally, it is interesting to determine the expected values for transport reliability and energy consumption of the forward link when we assume that the maximum number of retransmissions approaches infinity. Obviously, in this case a packet will always be successfully transmitted over any link of non-zero quality.

$$R_{r_f}^{link} = lim_{r_f \to \infty} R_{r_f}^{link} = 1 \qquad (3.11)$$

Analogously, we have:

$$E_{r_f}^{link} = lim_{r_f \to \infty} E_{r_f}^{link} = \frac{e_f + pe_b}{pq} \qquad (3.12)$$

Implicit Acknowledgements

The broadcast nature of wireless networks allows reducing the energy consumption compared to the explicit acknowledgement scheme through the use of overhearing of forwarding packets. This is called the implicit acknowledgement scheme. When a node $i - 1$ receives a packet from node i, node $i - 1$ forwards it to the node $i - 2$. This forwarding transmission can be overheard by node i and, therefore, serves as an implicit acknowledgement to node i. If an implicit acknowledgement is not received by node i before the timeout occurs, it retransmits the packet. In the case of many-to-one routing, if node $i - 1$ is the base station, it must acknowledge the reception of the packet explicitly as it is the communication endpoint that does not forward the message. We assume that the base station is attached to a power supply and, therefore, the use of explicit acknowledgements in this case does not degrade the network lifetime.

The advantage of using implicit acknowledgements is reduced energy consumption as fewer messages are transmitted between the nodes of a link. However, the implicit acknowledgement scheme can only be used if a message from a source node is always forwarded along the path and no aggregation is performed.

When using the implicit acknowledgement scheme, it is possible that a packet forwarded by node $i - 1$ is successfully received at node $i - 2$ whereas the implicit acknowledgement is lost on the reverse link $\langle i - 1, i \rangle$. In this case, node i retransmits the packet after the timeout. Although node $i - 1$ has already forwarded the packet, this case requires node $i - 1$ to resend the packet again to acknowledge its reception to the sender. The latter triggers node $i - 2$ to do the same, since it assumes that node $i - 1$ has missed the implicit acknowledgement of node $i - 2$. These unnecessary retransmissions continue along the path down to the sink. This is called the avalanche effect [RLD$^+$08, LRC$^+$08].

The avalanche effect occurs, because node $i - 2$ does not know that node i did not receive its implicit acknowledgement and node $i - 1$ resends the packet only to inform node i. There are several ways to avoid this [RLD$^+$08]. One way is to use an orientation bit in the packets which allows distinguishing between the retransmission of a packet as an acknowledgement in downstream direction on the one hand, and the retransmission in upstream direction caused by the loss of an implicit acknowledgement on the other hand. If the destination address of the next hop is part of the packet, this address can also be used to explicitly address either node $i - 2$ or node i. Another option is to use a combination of implicit and explicit acknowledgements. The first forwarding of a packet at node $i - 1$ is used as an implicit acknowledgement at node i. All further receptions of the same packet at node $i - 1$ from node i trigger an explicit acknowledgement of this packet in downstream direction.

We model the link characteristics of the implicit acknowledgement scheme assuming the use of one of the discussed methods to avoid the avalanche effect. The applied method determines the value of e_b: it corresponds to either the cost of sending an explicit acknowledgement or the cost of sending an implicit one, i.e., a full packet.

As for explicit acknowledgements, we consider three cases: Node i does not retransmit packets, the number of retransmissions is limited to some finite value or the number of retransmissions is unlimited.

Case 1: No retransmissions $(r_f = 1)$

This case corresponds to not using acknowledgements at all and providing a simple best-effort service. If node i does not use retransmissions, the transport reliability of the link is equal to the probability of a successful packet reception over the link $\langle i, i-1 \rangle$.

$$R_{r_f}^{link} = p \tag{3.13}$$

In contrast to the explicit acknowledgments scheme, implicit acknowledgements do not incur any overhead if no retransmissions are used. Therefore, the energy consumption of the link corresponds to the energy spent by node i to send a packet.

$$E_{r_f}^{link} = e_f \tag{3.14}$$

Case 2: Limited number of transmissions $(r_f \ll \infty)$

Obviously, using implicit instead of explicit acknowledgements does not change the transport reliability of the forward link. Therefore, we have:

$$R_{r_f}^{link} = \sum_{k=1}^{r_f} p(1-p)^{k-1} = 1 - (1-p)^{r_f} \tag{3.15}$$

Although the use of implicit acknowledgements influences the total expected energy consumption of the link, only the first successful transmission profits from the use of implicit acknowledgements. The link energy consumption using implicit acknowledgements corresponds to the energy consumption of the explicit acknowledgement scheme minus the cost for acknowledging the first successful transmission. We have:

$$E_{r_f}^{link} = \sum_{k=0}^{r_f-1} (1-pq)^k (e_f + pe_b) - e_b p \sum_{k=0}^{r_f-1} (1-p)^k = \tag{3.16}$$

$$(e_f + pe_b) \frac{1 - (1-pq)^{r_f}}{pq} - e_b(1 - (1-p)^{r_f})$$

Case 3: Infinite number of transmissions ($r_f \to \infty$)

As for explicit acknowledgements, we additionally consider the case when the number of retransmissions is not limited. This results in the following estimates for the forward link characteristics:

$$R_{r_f}^{link} = lim_{r_f \to \infty} R_{r_f}^{link} = 1 \tag{3.17}$$

$$E_{r_f}^{link} = lim_{r_f \to \infty} E_{r_f}^{link} = \frac{e_f + pe_b}{pq} - e_b \tag{3.18}$$

Lazy Acknowledgements

When using the previous two acknowledgement schemes a sender detects packet losses by waiting for an acknowledgement from the receiver. The authors of [QC06] showed that these timeout-based solutions fail to utilize a path to its full capacity. Unfortunately, both forward links and reverse links are not perfect. Therefore, the sender wastes bandwidth by retransmitting packets that have already been successfully delivered. To avoid this problem, the authors of [QC06] propose making the receiver responsible for detecting packet losses and requesting retransmissions from the sender. In this thesis, we call this approach the *lazy* acknowledgement scheme.

In the lazy acknowledgements scheme, the sender does not manage any time-outs. The loss of a packet is detected by the receiver when the next packet (e.g., with a higher sequence number) is received. In this case, the receiver node $i - 1$ notifies the sender node i by a retransmission request packet (RRP) of the lost packet. As the reverse link $\langle i - 1, i \rangle$ is not perfect, node $i - 1$ may have to apply retransmissions of RRP packets until it recovers from the packet loss or reaches the maximum number of transmissions for RRP. While saving energy and reducing the delay, the lazy acknowledgement scheme requires the temporary buffering of packets on the nodes to maintain the correct sequence of packets at the receiver. And, similar to the implicit acknowledgement scheme, the applicability is limited and requires to use application knowledge and that the communication pattern exhibits stream-like properties. It cannot be used for sending a single packet.

For analysing this scheme we assume that node i retransmits a packet on every reception of an RRP from node $i - 1$, and node $i - 1$ uses at most r_b RRP transmissions to notify node i of a transmission failure. Therefore, the *receiver* defines the maximum number of retransmissions since the receiver is also responsible for detecting packet losses. Note that, compared to previous schemes, $r_b = 0$ now signifies that no retransmissions of a lost packet are available. Analogously to the previous schemes, sending a packet requires e_f energy units and requesting a retransmission consumes e_b energy units for sending a retransmission request packet.

As for the previous schemes, three cases are considered: No retransmissions are allowed and, therefore, node $i - 1$ does not send any retransmission request packets; the number of retransmissions is limited to some finite value, and the number of retransmissions is unlimited.

Case 1: No retransmissions $(r_b = 0)$

In this simplest case, the expected transport reliability of the forward link is the same as for both previous models.

$$R_{r_b}^{link} = p \tag{3.19}$$

The energy consumption of a link consists of the energy required to send a packet and a RRP packet is not sent for lost packets.

$$E_{r_b}^{link} = e_f \tag{3.20}$$

Case 2: Limited number of transmissions $(0 < r_b \ll \infty)$

The first send along the forward link succeeds with probability p. Therefore, in $(1-p)$ cases, the node $i-1$ starts sending RRP packets as soon as it detects a packet loss. The kth retransmission of a lost packet succeeds with the probability $(1-pq)^{k-1}qp$: the previous $k-1$ transmissions were unsuccessful with the probability $(1 - pq)^{k-1}$ and the last transmission succeeded with the probability qp. Therefore, the expected value of the transport reliability $R_{r_b}^{link}$ is:

$$R_{r_b}^{link} = p + (1 - p) \sum_{k=1}^{r_b} (1 - pq)^{k-1} qp \tag{3.21}$$

$$= p + (1 - p)(1 - (1 - pq)^{r_b})$$

The energy consumption for the general case is calculated in a similar manner. The first transmission of a packet requires e_f energy units. If this transmission was unsuccessful (with probability $(1 - p)$), an RRP packet is sent. The transmission of the kth RRP packet and the resending of the data packet consume $(e_b + qe_p)(1 - pq)^{k-1}$ energy units. Therefore, we obtain:

$$E_{r_b}^{link} = e_f + (1 - p) \sum_{k=1}^{r_b} (e_b + qe_f)(1 - pq)^{k-1} \qquad (3.22)$$

$$= e_f + (1 - p)(e_b + qe_f) \frac{1 - (1 - pq)^{r_b}}{pq}$$

Case 3: Infinite number of transmissions $(r_b \to \infty)$

If node $i - 1$ allows an unlimited number of RRP transmissions, we obtain the following expected values for our link characteristics:

$$R_{r_b}^{link} = lim_{r_b \to \infty} R_{r_b}^{link} = 1 \qquad (3.23)$$

$$E_{r_b}^{link} = lim_{r_b \to \infty} E_{r_b}^{link} = \frac{e_f}{p} + \frac{e_b}{pq} - \frac{e_b}{q} \qquad (3.24)$$

The formulas introduced in this subsection show that the expected values for transport reliability and energy consumption differ considerably between different acknowledgement schemes. Additionally, our model of the link layer supports link asymmetry and considers different costs for sending packets and acknowledgements or RRP packets respectively.

The formulas modeling the acknowledgement schemes also allow calculating the expected number of packet transmissions: The values can be derived from the energy equations of the corresponding link layer model by setting $e_f = 1$ and $e_b = 0$. Similarly, if $e_f = 0$ and $e_b = 1$, we obtain the expected number of acknowledgements or RRP transmissions respectively.

In Table 3.1, we summarize the formulas for the different link layer acknowledgement schemes and the different cases.

In the following subsection we focus on evaluating the transport reliability and energy consumption as a path characteristic abstracting from the specific link layer model used.

Model/Case	Transport Reliability	Energy Consumption
Expl, $r_f = 1$	p	$e_f + pe_b$
Impl, $r_f = 1$	p	e_f
Lazy, $r_b = 0$	p	e_f
Expl, $r_f \ll \infty$	$1 - (1-p)^{r_f}$	$(e_f + pe_b)\frac{1-(1-pq)^{r_f}}{pq}$
Impl, $r_f \ll \infty$	$1 - (1-p)^{r_f}$	$(e_f + pe_b)\frac{1-(1-pq)^{r_f}}{pq}$ $-e_b(1 - (1-p)^{r_f})$
Lazy, $r_b \ll \infty$	$p + (1-p)(1 - (1-pq)^{r_b})$	$e_f + (1-p)(e_b + qe_f) \times \frac{1-(1-pq)^{r_b}}{pq}$
Expl, $r_f \to \infty$	1	$\frac{e_f + pe_b}{pq}$
Impl, $r_f \to \infty$	1	$\frac{e_f + pe_b}{pq} - e_b$
Lazy, $r_b \to \infty$	1	$\frac{e_f}{p} + \frac{e_b}{pq} - \frac{e_b}{q}$

Table 3.1: Overview of the link layer model

3.3.2 Path Layer Modeling

Transmitting a packet over a link can be modeled as a Bernoulli trial. However, transmitting a packet over a path is not a Bernoulli process, because if the packet is lost on one of the links, it is not forwarded any further. This fact is the basis of the path model and explains why the forward and reverse paths are not equal when assuming a finite number of retransmissions.

Let us assume that a packet originates at node n and is to be forwarded to the sink 0 using some path d. The forward link qualities along the path are $R_n^{link}, R_{n-1}^{link}, \ldots R_1^{link}$ and the energy spent to transmit a packet over each link is $E_n^{link}, E_{n-1}^{link} \ldots E_1^{link}$. These expected values are calculated as explained in the previous section depending on the link properties and the underlying link layer acknowledgement scheme used.

The expected forward transport reliability of the path is the product of the forward transport reliability of the links that form this path:

$$R^{path} = \prod_{i=1}^{n} R_i^{link} \qquad (3.25)$$

The expected energy consumption is calculated as follows: The node n on the path first transmits the packets over the link $\langle n, n-1 \rangle$ which consumes E_n^{link} energy units. However, only a fraction of R_n^{link} packets are expected to successfully reach the node $n - 1$. Only this portion of the packets require further forwarding and, therefore, result in additional energy consumption. This process is applied recursively. Therefore, we have the following expected energy consumption:

$$E^{path} = E_n^{link} + R_n^{link}(E_{n-1}^{link} + R_{n-1}^{link}(\ldots + R_2^{link}(E_1^{link}))) \tag{3.26}$$

The calculation of the expected value for transport reliability shows that there is no difference in the sequence of links the path comprises. However, the expected energy consumption of the path does depend on the sequence of links on the path. The intuition behind this behavior is that if a packet is lost it is cheaper (requires less energy) to lose it at the beginning of the path than losing it further down along the path. Therefore, even paths with the same transport reliability may differ significantly with respect to their energy costs. This important insight is the basis for the development of the energy-efficient routing metric presented in the next section.

3.4 Energy Efficient Routing Metrics

After introducing the network model, the algebra for routing metrics and an overview of existing metrics for WSNs as well as the link layer and path model, we now discuss energy efficiency with respect to routing metrics. We provide a definition of different possible optimization goals, examine the associated challenges and show the deficiencies of existing routing metrics in this regard.

3.4.1 Energy Efficiency

Although a number of papers have proposed using the metrics discussed above for energy-efficient routing and *EPB* was developed exactly for this goal, the term energy efficiency itself has not been defined properly. *Energy efficiency* is a well-defined term in physics expressing the ratio of output energy over input energy. Following the spirit of this definition, we propose to define energy efficiency of routing as the ratio of expected transport reliability over expected energy consumption:

$$\frac{Exp\,(Transport\,Reliability)}{Exp\,(Energy\,Consumption)} \to max \tag{3.27}$$

The inverse of this metric $\frac{Exp\ (Energy\ Consumption)}{Exp\ (Transport\ Reliability)} \rightarrow min$ expresses exactly the same behavior. The Energy per Bit metric tries to capture this meaning but fails due to shortcomings explained later.

Note that optimizing energy consumption alone without regarding the transport reliability is not a reasonable goal as this results in choosing very long hops providing low quality. Actually, the behavior of *SPF* approaches this optimization goal with devastating results concerning the packet loss rate [CACM03, GYHG04].

In contrast to energy consumption, the exclusive focus on optimizing transport reliability is a valid goal which is expressed by the *SR* and *SRQ* metrics. However, finding a balance between high quality and low cost paths and choosing cheaper paths when considering paths of the same quality is the ultimate goal of energy efficient routing metrics.

3.4.2 Shortcomings of Existing Routing Metrics

One radical difference of routing in wireless sensor networks compared to routing in more traditional and ad-hoc networks is the inherent unreliability of the packet transmission even from the perspective of the application layer. The majority of applications outside of the sensor networks domain assume a reliable transport medium that is usually provided by a combination of high quality links with a reliable transport layer like TCP. However, this basic premise does not hold in wireless sensor networks. For a large portion of applications the importance of individual packets diminishes in comparison to the sink receiving at least a significant fraction of all generated packets for an extended period of time. However, this important difference has a strong impact on the calculation of the energy consumption of a path (cf. above) and, therefore, on the energy efficiency. Nevertheless, this principle is not included in existing metrics which results in three shortcomings common to the previous approaches and motivates the need for an accurate modeling of packet routing both at the link and the routing layer.

First, we motivate regarding the consideration of the two directions of a data flow which is missing in such metrics as *SPF*, *SR*, *SRQ*, *ETX* and *EPB*. The motivating example is taken from our previous work [SML+06].

Second, since in any routing protocol the maximum number of retransmissions is limited, accurate modeling of the link layer with respect to this parameter is required. The routing metrics *ETX* and *EBP* assume that a packet always reaches the sink, and, therefore, that the maximum number of retransmissions is unlimited. However, packet losses are an integral part

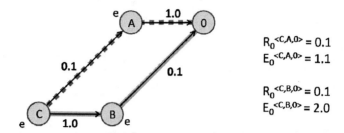

$$R_0^{<C,A,0>} = 0.1$$
$$E_0^{<C,A,0>} = 1.1$$

$$R_0^{<C,B,0>} = 0.1$$
$$E_0^{<C,B,0>} = 2.0$$

Figure 3.2: Motivating example for including the direction of the data flow in the metric

of wireless sensor networks and must be included in the model. We show an example, where the paths chosen by *ETX* or *EBP* deviate from the optimal ones due to the absence of a proper parameterization.

Finally, we motivate the inclusion of the underlying link-layer acknowledgement model to improve the quality of the metrics.

Direction of the Data Flow

Many existing routing metrics construct paths regardless of the direction of the data flow (*SPF, SR, SRQ, ETX* and *EPB*). However, in many WSN scenarios, the routing algorithms for data acquisition construct paths from any node in the network to the sink (many-to-one). The dissemination of messages (one-to-many), in contrast, is usually achieved by flooding or a derivative using broadcast as the underlying communication primitive (e.g., Trickle [LPCS04]).

The following example which we have taken from our previous work [SML+06] is used to illustrate the importance of incorporating the direction of the data flow into the path selection metric. Fig. 3.2 shows a network of four nodes where node C tries to send 100 data packets to the sink node (node 0). There are two possible routes to reach the sink, either via node A or via node B. The links $\langle C, A \rangle$, $\langle B, 0 \rangle$ and $\langle A, 0 \rangle$, $\langle C, B \rangle$ have link qualities of 1.0 and 0.1 respectively (Forward and backward links are assumed to have the same link qualities). We assume that all nodes spend an equal amount of energy e for each attempt to transmit a packet over any available link. No retransmissions of lost packets are performed.

The *SPF*, *SR*, *SRQ*, *EPB* and *ETX* metrics all consider both paths to be equal in terms of their quality. The *SPF* metric assigns a value of 2 to both paths which corresponds to two hops to the sink. The *SPF(t)* metric either produces the same result as *SPF* or fails to find any route, if it blacklists links with a link quality of 0.1. The *SR* metric computes the same value for the end-to-end success rate of both paths $(0.1 \cdot 1.0 = 0.1)$. Thus, only 10 packets are expected to reach the sink. The *SRQ* metric assigns a value of $0.1 \cdot 0.1 \cdot 1.0 \cdot 1.0 = 0.01$ to both paths. The *ETX* metric estimates the number of transmissions to be $\frac{1}{0.1} + \frac{1}{1.0} = 11$ for both paths. Finally, the *EPB* metric values for both paths are $\frac{1}{0.1} + \frac{1-0.1}{0.1 \cdot 0.1} + \frac{1}{1} + \frac{1-1.0}{1.0 \cdot 1.0} = 101$ (assuming $\lambda = 1$).

Obviously, the expected number of packets to reach the sink is the same for both paths. However, the energy spent by the sensor network if the first route is selected is nearly twice as much as the energy spent in the case of using the second route. The reason for this is that node A is expected to receive only 10% of the 100 packets sent by node C and, therefore, spends only 10e energy units for forwarding these 10 packets to node 0. The expected energy consumption of the path over node A is, therefore, 110e: 100e spent by node C and 10e spent by node A for forwarding. The route over node B is much more expensive: Node B is expected to receive all packets sent by node C and tries forwarding all of them to node 0. Although still only 10 packets are expected to arrive at the sink, the path energy consumption is 200e: 100e spent by node C for sending and 100e spent by node B for forwarding.

Differentiating between the path directions is based on this intuition: If a packet is lost, it is better to lose it as soon as possible and save the energy spent by other nodes trying to forward it. Moreover, this example also shows that it is necessary to include the energy consumption in the routing metric.

Finite Number of Transmissions

If we assume that the nodes in a WSN operate at different transmission power levels and use different maximum numbers of retransmissions, the energy demands of different paths from a node to the sink might differ considerably. The *SR*, *SRQ*, *ETX* and *EPB* routing metrics take none of these parameters into account. *SR* assumes that every packet is transmitted only once. *SRQ* incorporates the probability of an acknowledgement arrival into the metric value regardless of the maximum number of retransmissions available at every node. *ETX* and *EPB* assume that the number of transmissions is unlimited and, therefore, consider reliable transmission semantics.

We argue that including the number of possible retransmissions into the

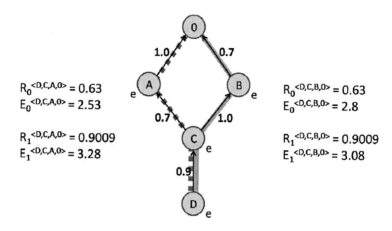

$R_0^{<D,C,A,0>} = 0.63$
$E_0^{<D,C,A,0>} = 2.53$

$R_1^{<D,C,A,0>} = 0.9009$
$E_1^{<D,C,A,0>} = 3.28$

$R_0^{<D,C,B,0>} = 0.63$
$E_0^{<D,C,B,0>} = 2.8$

$R_1^{<D,C,B,0>} = 0.9009$
$E_1^{<D,C,B,0>} = 3.08$

Figure 3.3: Motivating example for including the maximum number of transmissions in the metric

routing metric improves the path selection decision. The example in Fig. 3.3 illustrates this with a sample topology with link qualities and link energy consumption values assigned as shown in the figure. For the sake of simplicity, we assume that $p = q$ and $e_b = 0$ for this example. Consider the two possible paths from node D to the sink 0 over node A or node B respectively. First, we assume that the number of transmissions is limited to 1. Then, $R_{r=1}^{\langle D,C,A,0\rangle} = R_{r=1}^{\langle D,C,B,0\rangle} = 0.63$. The corresponding energy consumption then is $E_{r=1}^{\langle D,C,A,0\rangle} = 2.53$ and $E_{r=1}^{\langle D,C,B,0\rangle} = 2.8$. If no retransmissions of lost packets are allowed, the first path is cheaper than the second having the same expected transport reliability. Now consider the case where it is possible to retransmit a packet once: $R_{r=2}^{\langle D,C,A,0\rangle} = R_{r=2}^{\langle D,C,B,0\rangle} = 0.9009$, $E_{r=2}^{\langle D,C,A,0\rangle} = 3.28$, $E_{r=2}^{\langle D,C,B,0\rangle} = 3.08$. In this case, the transport reliability remains unchanged. However, the second path is now cheaper with respect to energy consumption.

This example shows that the choice of the best path depends on the maximum number of transmissions, which is limited for every routing protocol and, therefore, must be included in the routing metric.

Link Layer Acknowledgements

Routing metrics often operate on a weighted graph model of the sensor network while ignoring the underlying link layer protocols used. Although such routing metrics support the goal of minimizing the dependencies between individual layers of the protocol stack, it has been shown in a number of works (e.g., [LMMR05]) that cross-layer interactions are crucial in WSNs and allow for further optimizations of the network performance.

The link layer acknowledgement schemes influence the transport reliability of wireless links and define how much energy is spent by nodes for a packet transmission. As both characteristics are equally important for constructing energy-efficient routing metrics, link layer acknowledgements should be included in the considered metrics.

3.4.3 Optimality

As discussed in Section 3.2.2, optimality is one of the main criteria for evaluating routing metrics. In this section, we discuss optimality not with respect to a routing metric but more general with respect to an optimization goal. This goal can then be directly expressed by a metric.

Optimizing for transport reliability alone is optimal, because the best path of a parent is also the best subpath for any descendant in the tree. However, optimizing for energy efficiency is unfortunately not optimal, i.e., it is not possible in general to construct a routing tree such that the path from every node to the base station is optimal with respect to energy consumption. Only if every node chooses its path independently of the other nodes, optimality can be guaranteed. However, this requires a source routing approach and does not result in a routing tree.

The problem lies in the missing left-isotonicity of energy-efficiency as an optimization goal. This stems from the fact that a better path for a node does not necessarily result in a better path for its descendants.

In Fig. 3.4 we show an example topology that results in non-optimal behavior. We consider link transport reliabilities and link energy consumptions assigned as illustrated in the figure. To calculate the path characteristics, we use Equation 3.25 for the transport reliability and Equation 3.26 for the energy consumption. We use energy efficiency (EE) as defined by Equation 3.27 to choose between paths. In this case, for node C the path $\langle C, A, 0 \rangle$ with path characteristics $R^{\langle C,A,0 \rangle} = 0.36$, $E^{\langle C,A,0 \rangle} = 5.65$, $EE = 0.064$ is optimal and is preferred over the path $\langle C, B, 0 \rangle$ ($R^{\langle C,B,0 \rangle} = 0.4$,

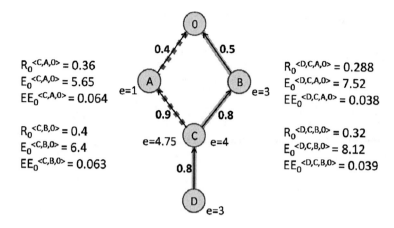

Figure 3.4: Non-optimality of energy efficiency as a routing goal

$E^{\langle C,B,0 \rangle} = 6.4$, $EE = 0.063$). However, for its child node D, the path $\langle D,C,A,0 \rangle$ ($R^{\langle D,C,A,0 \rangle} = 0.288$, $E^{\langle D,C,A,0 \rangle} = 7.52$, $EE = 0.038$) is worse than $\langle D,C,B,0 \rangle$ ($R^{\langle D,C,B,0 \rangle} = 0.32$, $E^{\langle D,C,B,0 \rangle} = 8.12$, $EE = 0.039$). Nevertheless, the child is forced to pick the path over its parent node C, although there is a better path for node D in the network.

Although optimality is impossible to achieve for energy efficiency as an optimization goal, we will show later that the routing tree generated by our metric still performs better than the existing ones.

3.5 The Routing Metric GEM^x

In previous work [SML$^+$06], we have defined the routing metric GEM (**G**ain per **E**nergy **M**etric) based on the following optimization criteria:

$$\text{GEM} = \frac{Exp(Gain)_r}{Exp(Energy)_r} \rightarrow \textbf{max} \qquad (3.28)$$

where r is the maximum number of transmissions and $Exp(Gain)$ and $Exp(Energy)$ are R^{path} and E^{path} respectively derived in a similar manner as discussed in this chapter but using a simplified model for the implicit acknowledgement scheme.

GEM optimizes the ratio between the expected transport reliability of a path and its expected energy consumption. Therefore, GEM selects routes with the best performance-price ratio. However, GEM does not allow to express a "more important than" relation between transport reliability and energy consumption, which is crucial if specified quality of service (QoS) requirements with regard to transport reliability or lifetime requirements are not met.

Therefore, for the work presented in this thesis, we have modified GEM by introducing the parameter x which is a weighting factor between the path transport reliability and the energy consumption. This modified routing metric GEM^x is tunable and has the following form:

$$\text{GEM}^x = \frac{(R^{path})^x}{E^{path}} \rightarrow \textbf{max} \qquad (3.29)$$

where R^{path} and E^{path} are defined by the model described in this chapter. GEM^x has the following features:

Generality: GEM^x covers the most popular energy-efficient routing metrics: GEM, ETX, SR and EPB. We show in the following which parameter settings and simplifications of the model must be applied to GEM^x in order to obtain the existing metrics. In Fig. 3.5 we summarize the interrelations between these metrics and GEM^x.

If $x \rightarrow \infty$, the comparison of two paths by GEM$^\infty$ results in the same selection as by using the $\frac{R^{path}}{(E^{path})^0}$ metric where the path selection is indifferent to the expected energy consumption. Therefore, for $x \rightarrow \infty$, GEM^x behaves similar to SR in the sense that the path providing the best expected transport reliability is chosen. However, the metric is parameterized with the limited maximum number of transmissions and models the link layer correctly. By keeping this parameterization, we can eliminate the weaknesses of SR mentioned in Sections 3.4.2 to 3.4.2 and introduce the improved version $SR_r = \prod_{i=1}^{n} R_i^{link} \rightarrow \textbf{max}$ which uses accurate modeling of the transport reliability by considering the underlying link layer scheme. Most importantly, SR_r takes into account that the maximum number of retransmissions is limited and may even vary from node to node. Therefore, SR_r incorporates the direction of the data flow.

If $x = 1$, GEM^x corresponds to the three existing energy-efficient (optimizing the performance-price ratio) metrics ETX_{er}, GEM and EBP_r for explicit, implicit and lazy acknowledgement schemes respectively. ETX_{er} and EBP_r are defined by means of the Equations 3.9 & 3.10 and 3.21 &

Figure 3.5: Spectrum of routing metrics covered by GEM^x

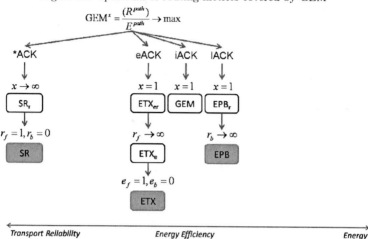

3.22 respectively. Compared to the original metrics ETX and EPB, ETX_{er} and EPB_r consider that the maximum number of transmissions is limited. ETX_{er} additionally models the actual amount of energy required to send a packet and an explicit acknowledgement. Therefore, it supports different transmission power levels along the path. Note that the original EPB metric already considers this by including $\lambda = \frac{e_b}{e_f}$ in its definition. The metrics ETX_{er} and EBP_r correspond to improved versions of ETX and EPB that do not suffer from the weaknesses described in Section 3.4.2. If we assume that the number of possible transmissions is infinite for both ETX_{er} and EBP_r, we obtain the ETX_e and EBP metrics. Here, ETX_e is an improved version of ETX which takes the energy consumption of sending a packet and an explicit acknowledgement into account:

$$\text{ETX}_e = \frac{1}{\sum_{i=1}^{n} \frac{e_f + p_i e_b}{p_i q_{i-1}}} \rightarrow \mathbf{max} \qquad (3.30)$$

If in ETX_e we set $e_f = 1$ and $e_b = 0$, we obtain the number of expected transmissions optimized by ETX. Note that all ETX and EPB derivatives are inverted compared to GEM^x. However, inverse versions of metrics exhibit the same behavior as the original ones, because only the result of a comparison between different paths is relevant and not the absolute values calculated by the metric.

All discussed routing metrics either optimize the performance-price ratio (*ETX*, *GEM*, *EBP* and variations) or the transport reliability (*SR* and variations). As has been shown above, optimizing only with respect to energy consumption is not a reasonable goal.

We have evaluated the benefit of the proposed improvements. We compared the routing metrics SR_r, ETX_{er} and EBP_r to their original versions. SR_r performs 1-6% better than *SR* with respect to path transport reliability on networks of 10 hops. ETX_{er} is up to 85% more energy efficient compared to the original *ETX* metric when using the explicit acknowledgement scheme if no retransmissions of lost packets are allowed and up to 5% more efficient when the maximum number of transmissions is limited to $r_f = 3$. EBP_r in combination with lazy acknowledgements is up to 7% more energy-efficient if no retransmissions are allowed and only up to 1% if their maximum number is limited to $r_b = 2$. We used the same simulation settings to obtain these values as in the evaluation section of this chapter.

Parameterization: The expected path transport reliability (R^{path}) and the expected path resource demands (E^{path}) are directly included in the target metric and any changes to these characteristics influence the GEM^x path estimation value. Thus, GEM^x is sensitive to changes of the maximum number of transmissions r as well as to the changes of the transmission power level on every node. A change of the TPL can result in different link characteristics e_f, e_b, p and q whereas the parameter r is explicitly included in the link layer model.

Adaptation: In principle, it is possible to tune the value of the parameter x in order to specify the relative importance of transport reliability and energy characteristics in the following way:

$$\begin{cases} 0 \le x < 1 & \text{energy is more important than gain,} \\ x = 1 & \text{energy and gain are equally important.} \\ 1 < x < \infty & \text{gain is more important than energy,} \end{cases} \qquad (3.31)$$

However, GEM^x is not strictly left-monotonic if x is less than 1:

$$\frac{(R^{path})^x}{E^{path}} > \frac{(R^{path})^x (R^{link})^x}{E^{link} + R^{link} E^{path}}$$

Therefore,

$$E^{link} + E^{path} R^{link} (1 - (R^{link})^{x-1}) > 0$$

The last inequality only holds for $1 \leq x < \infty$. However, since increasing the importance of good transport reliability at the expense of an increased energy consumption is the usual tuning direction, the restriction $x \geq 1$ is not considered critical. Therefore, GEM^x can be adapted only in the more important direction of preferring gain over energy.

The tuning of the parameter x has the following properties:

Property 1 Let d_1 be the path from node n to the sink 0 built by GEM^x where x_i is the value x for each node i. If node k along d_1 increases x_k, then there exists an assignment $x_{k+1} \ldots x_n$ which leads to the selection of a path d_2 so that $R^{d_2} \geq R^{d_1}$.

Property 2 Let d_1 be the path from node n to the sink 0 built by GEM^x given x_i for each node i. If node k along d_1 increases its transmission power level, then there exists an assignment $x_{k+1} \ldots x_n$ which leads to the formation of a path d_2, so that $R^{d_2} \geq R^{d_1}$.

Property 3 Let d_1 be the path from node n to the sink 0 built by GEM^x given x_i for each node i. If node k along d_1 increases the number of retransmissions, then there exists an assignment $x_{k+1} \ldots x_n$ which leads to the formation of a path d_2, so that $R^{d_2} \geq R^{d_1}$.

These properties are important to guarantee that measures taken to improve the transport reliability – increasing x, TPL and/or the maximum number of retransmissions – do actually result in an increased path reliability. This is not necessarily true for GEM, because the optimization goal is energy efficiency (in contrast to gain) and all discussed methods increase transport reliability as well as energy consumption.

Maximum network reliability: Consider a static network such that every node has a fixed transmission power level and a fixed maximum number of transmissions. For every node, there is maximum value for the transport reliability which can be obtained. The *maximum network reliability* is reached if all nodes choose a path that provides the maximum transport reliability. This is the optimization goal of SR_r and, as this metric is consistent and optimal, the constructed routing tree provides the maximum network reliability.

From the perspective of path lengths, shorter paths tend to be of bad quality because longer hops over bad quality links have to be used. However, there is also a maximum path length beyond which longer paths do not increase transport reliability any more but, in contrast, decrease the quality again.

On the one hand, GEM^x for $x = 1$ optimizes the ratio between transport reliability and energy consumption and, therefore, prefers shorter energy-efficient paths. On the other hand, reducing the influence of the energy component by increasing x corresponds to preferring more reliable links which results in longer but higher quality paths. The upper bound path reliability is reached for GEM^x, $x \rightarrow \infty$ which approaches its asymptote SR_r. We will show in the evaluation section how the tuning of x changes the behavior of GEM^x and increases the similarity to SR_r.

Awareness of Energy Consumption: Due to the accurate modeling of the link-layer acknowledgement scheme and the energy consumption of a path, GEM^x is energy-aware. Although ETX and EBP also take energy consumption into account, the underlying models for these metrics are less precise and rely on unrealistic assumptions, e.g., that the maximum number of transmissions is unlimited.

Accumulation: In order to calculate the value of GEM^x, there is no need to have global knowledge about the network topology or the path. GEM^x selects the route based on the accumulated values for the expected path transport reliability and the energy consumption propagated by each node starting from the sink. Equation 3.26 shows that this is also possible for energy consumption.

Blacklisting and Link Asymmetry: Similarly to other metrics (except SPF), GEM^x obviates the necessity of blacklisting, and, therefore, accounts for a wide range of link loss ratios and even the existence of asymmetric links.

Routing Tree Structure: Limiting the maximum number of transmissions results in different forward path and backward path energy consumptions. The rationale behind this property is that if a packet has to be lost, it is better to lose it as soon as possible (see Section 3.4.2). This fact influences the tree structure defined by GEM^x. The nodes that are far away from the sink have a tendency to select the nodes at a large distance for data forwarding whereas the nodes in the vicinity of the sink tend to select high quality links to minimize the risk of losing a packet. This feature results from including energy costs directly into the metric.

3.6 Analysis of Routing Metrics

In this section we use formal methods for analyzing all routing metrics presented in this chapter and classify them based on this analysis. We use two analysis schemes: First, we investigate the constructed routing trees for being consistent, optimal and loop-free. Second, we discuss the changes of the routing trees when retransmissions and TPL control schemes are applied.

3.6.1 Consistency, Optimality, Loop-freeness

We analyze all considered routing metrics with regard to them being consistent, optimal and loop-free. All additive metrics, i.e., *SPF*, *SPF(t)*, *ETX*, *EBP* are both strictly left-isotonic and strictly left-monotonic. GEM^x is left-monotonic for $x \geq 1$ (see Section 3.5) but not left-isotonic in general. Only special cases of GEM^x for $x \rightarrow \infty$, *SR* and the special cases for $x = 1$ which additionally assume an unlimited maximum number of retransmissions, *ETX* and *EPB* are left-isotonic but not GEM^x in general. Therefore, in contrast to the other metrics, GEM^x is not optimal in the general case. This means that although the optimization goal is energy-efficiency, the paths in the resulting routing tree are not guaranteed to be optimal for all nodes in the network. However, as discussed in Section 3.4, this is a limitation of energy efficiency as an optimization goal and not of the metric itself. Although all discussed routing metrics have been proposed for minimizing energy consumption and, therefore, are called energy-efficient, the optimization functions which define the resulting routing tree differ widely. For example, *SR* and *SRQ* optimize the transport reliability alone which only influences the energy consumption in a very indirect way. *ETX* optimizes the throughput by minimizing the expected number of transmissions along the path which is only related to the energy consumption of the path. *EBP* reduces the expected energy per bit characteristic which is a very good mapping of energy efficiency of the path and suffers only from considering retransmissions to be an unlimited resource. Although simplified models and unrealistic assumptions obscure the problem regarding optimality for energy-efficient routing, an accurate modeling of transport reliability and energy consumption coupled with a proper parameterization using the number of available retransmissions and the transmission power level considerably improve the performance of the routing metrics.

Although being both left-monotonic and strictly left-isotonic , SR and SRQ often result in cycles as soon as the network is dynamic due to the absence

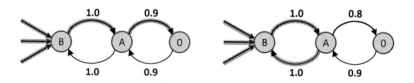

Figure 3.6: Loops in a routing tree caused by the SR and the SRQ metrics

Routing Metric	Consistency	Optimality	Loop-freeness
SPF	+	+	+
SR	-(+)	-(+)	-(+)
SRQ	-(+)	-(+)	-(+)
ETX	+	+	+
EPB	+	+	+
GEM^x	+	-	+

Table 3.2: Classification of routing metrics with respect to consistency, optimality and loop-freeness

of *strict* left-monotonicity. In Fig. 3.6 we show an example of a topology for which SR and SRQ result in routing loops once the network topology changes. The values of the transport reliability of the including link-layer calculations are assigned as shown in the figure. The SR and SRQ metrics result in a tree in which node A chooses node 0 and node B chooses node 1 as their parent. If the link $\langle A, 0 \rangle$ breaks down or just degrades due to network dynamics, node A decides to pick node B as its parent which results in a routing cycle. The reason for this is that the transport reliability of the link $\langle A, B \rangle$ equals 1.0 which does not decrease the value of the SR or the SRQ routing metric when appended to a path. Therefore, instead of a rapidly decreasing metric value when A chooses B and updates its metric and then B chooses A and updates its metric and so on, a seemingly stable path is created which results in a cycle. As soon as SR and SRQ result in routing cycles, they are neither consistent nor optimal nor loop-free. However, both metrics can be easily repaired to be strictly left-monotonic by setting $p, q \in [0, 1)$.

This problem shows that the definition of loop-freeness in [YW08] is incomplete: Although metrics that are left-monotonic build loop-free routing trees, changes in the underlying topology can result in loops. Since the authors discuss routing metrics in the context of multi-hop wireless networks, a fully static topology is not a reasonable assumption. Therefore, we corrected the conditions to include *strict* left-monotonicity for loop-freeness, consistency and optimality.

A summary of the characteristics of the metrics is presented in Table 3.2.

3.6.2 Sensitivity and Parameter Tuning

In this subsection we discuss energy-efficient routing metrics with respect to the tuning of two parameters: The transmission power level (TPL) and the maximum number of retransmissions. These parameters are important and can be used to manipulate the structure of the routing tree.

Tuning the TPL directly influences the number of neighbors of the node as well as the quality of communication with them. Increasing the TPL of a node does not decrease its communication quality with adjacent nodes [ZHKS04] but requires additional link energy. Therefore, it is generally possible to achieve a better transport reliability of the sensor network by increasing the value of the TPL while increasing the energy cost. Every radio chip has minimum and maximum values of its TPL setting and sensor networks often operate with the maximum TPL values for all active nodes.

Increasing the maximum number of retransmissions can further increase the quality of wireless links when the maximum TPL setting is reached or can be used as an alternative means to control the transport reliability. The maximum number of retransmissions can be set to any value during the network lifetime. This parameter is very convenient to use, as, in contrast to TPL, its influence on the transport reliability and the energy consumption of the link can be estimated quite accurately. Moreover, it does not result in network topology changes which in turn might lead to considerable changes to the overall structure of the routing tree.

We say that a routing metric is *sensitive* to a parameter P if changes to this parameter influence the decision made by the metric. If this is not the case, the routing metric is called *insensitive*. For example, all discussed routing metrics are sensitive to changes of the TPL, because these changes can influence the neighborhood relation between the nodes in the network. Changes to the number of retransmissions never lead to decision changes of insensitive routing metrics, which include *SPF*, *SR*, *SRQ*, *ETX* and *EBP*.

On the one hand, if a metric is insensitive to a parameter P, tuning of this parameter cannot damage the routing tree but might lead to non-optimal solutions. For example, an increase in the number of retransmissions in combination with an insensitive metric increases the transport reliability of the path. However, due to the insensitivity of the metric, another path with an even higher number of retransmissions may actually be optimal and might still be ignored. On the other hand, if the metric is sensitive to changes of P but not deterministic, this might result in unpredictable or unwanted changes of the routing tree structure. A well known example of such behavior

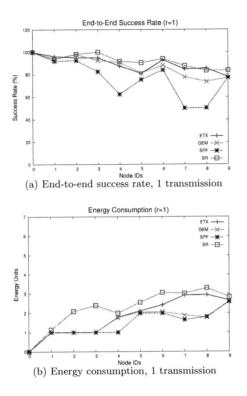

(a) End-to-end success rate, 1 transmission

(b) Energy consumption, 1 transmission

Figure 3.7: Real-world experiments: End-to-end success rate and distribution of the energy consumption in case of 1 transmission

is tuning of the TPL in order to improve the network transport reliability while having *SPF* as a metric. *SR*, *SRQ* and *GEM^x* behave predictably better in this case.

3.7 Evaluation

In this section we present evaluation results of the performance of the discussed routing metrics based on real-world experiments and simulations. The routing metrics *SPF*, *SR*, *ETX* and *GEM* were tested for constructing

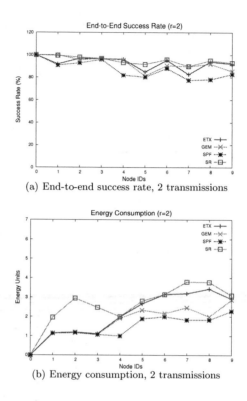

(a) End-to-end success rate, 2 transmissions

(b) Energy consumption, 2 transmissions

Figure 3.8: Real-world experiments: End-to-end success rate and distribution of the energy consumption in case of 2 transmissions

a routing tree on a small sensor network comprising 10 sensor nodes. The results of these experiments are presented in the next subsection. For better understanding the properties of routing metrics, we then present evaluation results of all the discussed routing metrics when simulating a sensor network with 225 sensor nodes. Moreover, we also simulated different acknowledgement schemes and studied the differences in the routing metric performance.

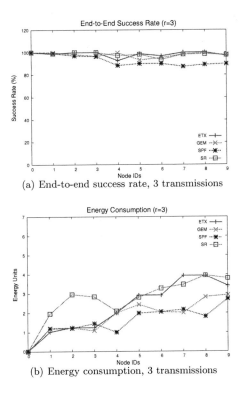

(a) End-to-end success rate, 3 transmissions

(b) Energy consumption, 3 transmissions

Figure 3.9: Real-world experiments: End-to-end success rate and distribution of the energy consumption in case of 3 transmissions

3.7.1 Real-world Experiments

The experiments presented in this subsection use 10 Tmote Sky motes based on the TI MSP430 microcontroller with a CC2420 radio module located in an office environment. The nodes where distributed in a room of 4.8 × 2.4 meters and the initial transmission power levels were set to one of the lowest possible values in oder to organize them into a multihop network.

There are some routing module settings that need to be mentioned. We have used a moving average to estimate the link quality with a window size of

10 (see [WTC03]). The acceptable missed value is equal to 5 packets, after which the entry is deleted from the routing table. The routing table size was set to 10, so that all the nodes had equal chances to be selected as parent for packet forwarding. Initially, all nodes communicate at power level $l_i = 2$ (range is [1..31]).

We have tested the three metrics *SPF*, *SR* and *ETX* from related work and compared them with *GEM*. In the first set of experiments we have evaluated the performance of these routing metrics for the case of 1, 2 and 3 maximum available transmissions and equally fixed transmission power levels. All merics were tested in combination with implicit link layer acknowledgement scheme. In our setting the experiment lasted 100 seconds and was repeated a total of five times. The graphs present the average of these five experiments.

As evaluation criteria we have included end-to-end packet success rate, which shows the percentage of successfully received packets from each node in the network; energy consumption of the selected path from each node; hop distribution along the path from each node to the sink; and route stability, i.e., the average number of parent changes during one experiment.

End-to-end Success Rate The three graphs in Fig. 3.7a), Fig. 3.8a) and Fig. 3.9a) show the percentage of packets which were successfully delivered to the sink node by each one of the nodes. The *SPF* metric has the worst behavior because it selects the minimal-hop paths and, therefore, the longest low quality links to route packets to the sink. *GEM* reflects energy consumption and gain as a simple ratio and shows nearly the same level of packet success rate as *ETX*. The reason for this is that the links from the transitional region are unstable, and, therefore, usually not considered for routing packets. This does not happen as a result of blacklisting, but rather because the packets are received accidentally via such links. The *SR* metric shows a good packet success rate, since it is targeted at maximizing this characteristic.

Energy Consumption The three graphs in Fig. 3.7b), Fig. 3.8b) and Fig. 3.9b) display the energy demands of using the selected path from each node. In all our examples we calculate the energy consumption of a path in energy units. One energy unit is the amount of energy needed to send a packet at the lowest possible transmission power level ($l = 1$). Using the Tmote Sky specification it is easy to estimate how many energy units are spent if communication takes place with higher power levels.

The energy consumption of paths obviously increases with each additional retransmission. *SPF* has the least energy demands in the case of 1 transmission. However, this is not true any more if the retransmission mechanism is available. This is because links with low qualities need additional send operations and, therefore, increase energy consumption of paths.

The *SR* metric shows the highest energy consumption for the paths from nearly every node. This is expected since it is the only metric that does not take energy consumption into account. *ETX* does it indirectly by estimating the number of transmissions and *SPF* does it by minimizing the number of hops.

ETX and *GEM* both take energy consumption into account (*ETX* is just a special case of *GEM*, when the number of transmissions approaches infinity). However, the distribution of energy consumption shows that considering an infinite number of transmissions still leads to energy losses (according to these experiments up to 30%), because *ETX* considers all paths to be undirected, which is not the case from the viewpoint of energy consumption of the path itself.

Hop Distribution The graph on the left-hand side of Fig. 3.10 reflects the depth of the routing tree. It shows the average number of hops needed by the selected path to route packets from each node. As expected the *SPF* metric selects the minimal hops paths to route packets whereas the *SR* metric selects the longest paths. *ETX* and *GEM* behave similarly.

Route Stability The average number of parent changes during one experiment is presented in the right graph of Fig. 3.10 and reflects the stability of the routing tree. As can be seen, the results have good correlation with hop distribution metrics. The paths selected by *SPF* metric are the most stable, whereas *SR* shows the least stability and, without considering the proposed in this chapter improvement, might lead to cycles in the routing tree. *ETX* and *GEM* behave similarly and have values between *SR* and *SPF*.

In general based on our tests, *GEM* shows a slightly worse end-to-end success rate than *SR* and *ETX*, but considerable gains in energy, that allow it to influence the success rate if needed by the application using helper techniques like the tuning of the maximum number of retransmissions and the transmission power level. Theoretically, since *GEM* tries to maximize the ratio of expected end-to-end packet success rate and energy consumption, the losses in end-to-end success rate are expected to be proportional to gains in energy. However, in practice, link qualities are not uniformly distributed. Links from the transitional region show high variations in link quality and, therefore, the link quality estimator degrades their value as candidates to be part of the selected route in stable scenarios. This makes *GEM* select good quality paths even for the case where retransmissions are not available, and show comparatively high energy savings.

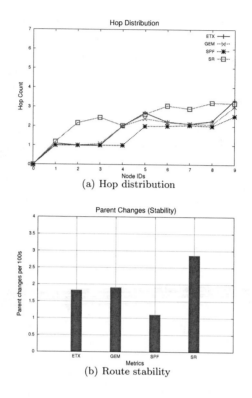

(a) Hop distribution

(b) Route stability

Figure 3.10: Real-world experiments: Hop distribution and routing tree stability

3.7.2 Simulation Results

In this subsection we evaluate the performance of energy-efficient routing metrics and analyze the results based on thorough simulations.

We simulated a sensor network consisting of 225 nodes organized in a 15×15 grid (to reduce variance) with the sink node placed in the middle. The cell spacing was set to 15.25 feet. We used the TinyOS LossyBuilder included in the TOSSIM package [LLWC03] for generating loss rates between each pair of nodes in the grid and simulated network topology changes with repeated calls of the generator (rounds). The tool models loss rates as observed in an experiment performed by [GKW⁺02].

Our goal is to evaluate the performance of routing metrics under different link layer acknowledgement schemes and different maximum number of retransmissions. The following evaluation criteria are considered:

- The *path transport reliability* for a node is the probability of successful packet delivery to the sink along the path constructed by a routing metric

- The *path energy consumption* for a node is the expected amount of energy consumed along this path

- The *path energy efficiency* for a node is the ratio between transport reliability and energy consumption

- The *load distribution* expresses the load on each node in the network including generated and forwarded traffic

- The *network gain* captures the number of messages that reach the sink node in one simulated round

- The *network lifetime* corresponds to the number of rounds the sensor network is functioning properly. The network lifetime can be determined by the point in time when first a node ceases to work or when the sink node is not connected to the rest of the network anymore and stops receiving messages from the sensor nodes.

Energy efficient routing metric are widely considered to increase network lifetime. In this section we will argue that it is generally not true and depends on a number of other factors the routing metric takes into account.

We start with an evaluation of the metrics' performance when using the explicit acknowledgements scheme. We simulated 1000 topologies to generate each plot.

In Fig. 3.11-Fig. 3.13 we plot the average path transport reliability, the average path energy consumption and the ratio between them over the geometric distance of the nodes to the sink. The distance is always expressed in grid cells, i.e., a distance of 1 corresponds to 15.25 feet. Fig. 3.11-3.13a) shows the case when no retransmissions of lost packets are applied and Fig. 3.11-3.13b) assumes that the maximum number of transmissions is limited to 3. We can observe that the *SR* metric achieves the best transport reliability. This was expected as the maximum reliability is the optimization goal of this metric and the resulting routing tree is optimal as shown above. However,

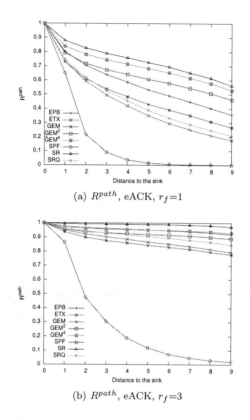

(a) R^{path}, eACK, $r_f=1$

(b) R^{path}, eACK, $r_f=3$

Figure 3.11: Simulation Results: Path transport reliability

SR routes are expensive. This is highlighted in the case when the maximum number of transmissions is limited to 3 which allows the other metrics to achieve similar transport reliability results. As expected and thoroughly discussed in [GYHG04], *SPF* provides unacceptably low transport reliability results as well as unacceptable gain per energy ratios plotted in Fig. 3.13.

Among the two energy-efficient routing metrics *ETX* and *EPB*, *ETX* outperforms *EPB* in these graphs when increasing the number of transmissions. The reason for this is that the explicit acknowledgement model is used which perfectly fits *ETX* whereas it does not work well with the design of *EPB*.

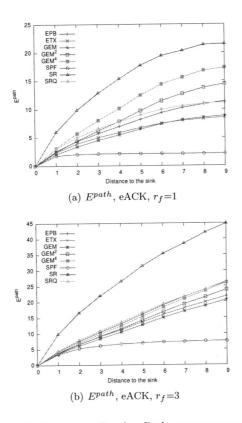

(a) E^{path}, eACK, $r_f=1$

(b) E^{path}, eACK, $r_f=3$

Figure 3.12: Simulation Results: Path energy consumption

We will observe the inverse result when the lazy acknowledgement link-layer model is used. Despite the lack of optimality, *GEM* shows the best gain per energy result (see Fig. 3.13) for any given maximum number of transmissions, since this is the value optimized by the metric. We evaluated the performance of GEM^x for $x = 1, 2, 4$. Increasing x puts more preference to transport reliability than to energy consumption of a path and, therefore, the metric approaches the behavior of SR_{r_i} when increasing x to infinity.

Note that the SR metric tends to choose longer paths than other metrics to provide a high transport reliability. Since *SR* is optimal with respect

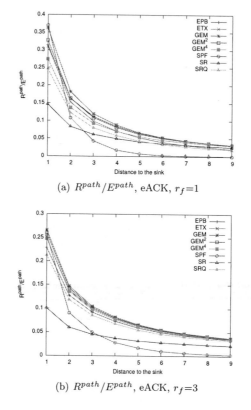

(a) R^{path}/E^{path}, eACK, $r_f=1$

(b) R^{path}/E^{path}, eACK, $r_f=3$

Figure 3.13: Simulation Results: Path gain per energy

to path gain, the resulting tree achieves the maximum network reliability. Thus, both shorter and longer paths lead to a worse transport reliability than achieved by *SR*.

Fig. 3.14a) shows the average load of the nodes depending on their distance to the sink. The load of a node is the expected amount of traffic that is routed over this particular node. It comprises the load generated by itself and the traffic received from descendant nodes in the routing tree that it has to forward. Additionally, from Fig. 3.14a) we can determine the amount of traffic that successfully reaches the sink node (out of the 225 packets that

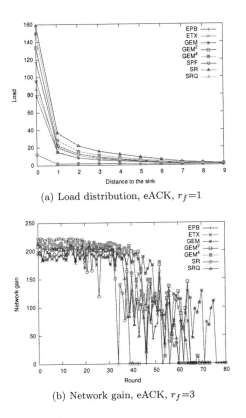

(a) Load distribution, eACK, $r_f=1$

(b) Network gain, eACK, $r_f=3$

Figure 3.14: Simulation Results: Load distribution and network gain

are generated during one simulation round).

Plots with higher maximum numbers of transmissions show the same tendencies and, therefore, we skip presenting them separately.

For the analysis shown in the next four graphs, we assigned 1000 energy units to every node in the network except for the sink node which possesses unlimited energy resources. Each trial consists of generating a topology, building a routing tree and simulating the sending of one packet from any reachable (part of the tree) node which depletes the energy available on the nodes. The simulation runs until there are no more nodes reachable from the sink in the network for 10 consecutive simulation rounds. The last 10 rounds are necessary due to network dynamics and the high variation of link qualities generated by the radio propagation simulator.

In Fig. 3.14b), we show the network gain and, therefore, network reachability, over time. When limiting the maximum number of packet transmissions to 3, the network survives as a whole for different numbers of rounds (depending on the routing metric) until the first node fails. Further reconfiguration of the routing tree leads to a fully connected structure with a smaller number of nodes being able to communicate with the sink. However, when the network looses connectivity, i.e., no node is reachable from the sink anymore, there are still around 170 nodes alive. The nodes around the sink handle more load than the nodes far away from the sink (see Fig. 3.14a)) and, therefore, are the first to run out of energy. This explains the relatively large ratio of nodes that are alive even when the network itself breaks down. *GEM* outperforms the other metrics due to better energy savings and provides reachability and network lifetime for the highest number of rounds. One can detect a considerable fluctuation of the network gain when the network runs out of energy. The reason for this behavior lies in a high variation of the link qualities between the sink node and the few remaining nodes that still possess energy and that are located further away from the sink than the forwarding nodes used before.

For the time the network stays reachable, we plot the expected number of messages that successfully reach the sink in every round in Fig. 3.14b). Notice a considerably lower deviation of network gain during the first rounds of simulation compared to the end. This stems from the fact that low quality links have a considerably higher variation than more reliable links which are relatively stable [GKW$^+$02, WTC03, ZG03]. Since nodes close to the sink run out of energy first, the routing tree has to include longer, low quality links in later rounds.

With the implicit acknowledgement link-layer model, all metrics show the same behavior with respect to path transport reliability as when the explicit acknowledgement link-layer model is used (see Equations 3.9 and 3.15). However, for the case of using lazy acknowledgements (see Fig. 3.18a)), all metrics show a slightly smaller transport reliability compared to the other two acknowledgement schemes. The explanation for this lies in the nature of lazy acknowledgements: For a sending node, the lost packet is resent only if the corresponding RRP is successfully received. On the one hand, in the lazy acknowledgement scheme there is a non-zero probability that the sending node is *not* notified about the loss of a packet which is not possible for implicit or explicit acknowledgements. On the other hand, it is not

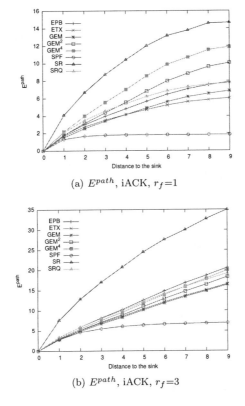

(a) E^{path}, iACK, $r_f=1$

(b) E^{path}, iACK, $r_f=3$

Figure 3.15: Simulation Results: Path energy consumption

possible that unnecessary retransmissions occur in the lazy acknowledgement scheme as is the case when using explicit or implicit acknowledgements. This saves energy compared to the other schemes (comparing the y-axis values in Fig. 3.12, Fig. 3.15 and Fig. 3.16).

The path energy consumption differs considerably among different link-layer acknowledgement schemes as plotted in Fig. 3.12, Fig. 3.15 and Fig. 3.16. With implicit acknowledgements, the energy cost of a path is reduced approximately by 22% compared to using the explicit acknowledgement scheme (see Fig. 3.15b)). If the communication pattern is accommodated by the lazy

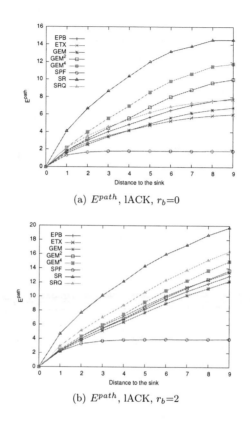

(a) E^{path}, lACK, r_b=0

(b) E^{path}, lACK, r_b=2

Figure 3.16: Simulation Results: Path energy consumption

acknowledgements scheme, this method is best for saving energy of the wireless nodes, as the paths are half as expensive (for 3 transmissions) as with explicit acknowledgements. Note that *EBP* better optimizes the energy usage when lazy acknowledgements are used than *ETX* (comparing Fig. 3.15 and Fig. 3.16) since it was designed for this link layer scheme.

Saving energy with the lazy acknowledgement link-layer scheme increases the lifetime of a sensor network. Comparing Fig. 3.14b) and Fig. 3.17 we show how the underlying link-layer acknowledgement scheme influences the expected network transport reliability. We can observe that having the same

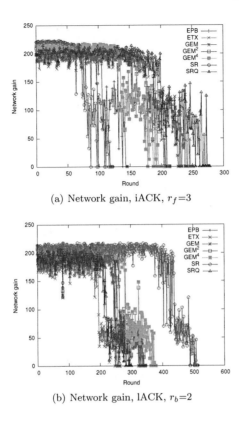

(a) Network gain, iACK, r_f=3

(b) Network gain, lACK, r_b=2

Figure 3.17: Simulation Results: Transport reliability for implicit and lazy acknowledgements

initial amount of energy of 1000 energy units leads to a network collapse using energy-efficient routing metrics after 60-80 rounds of simulation when the explicit acknowledgement scheme is used. The lifetime of the sensor network can be increased to 150-250 rounds under the same settings if the first acknowledgement is implicit whereas the use of lazy acknowledgements prolongs the network lifetime to 250-350 rounds.

Fig. 3.17b) shows an interesting property of the lazy link layer acknowledgements. Under this scheme, the routing metric *SR* which optimizes for-

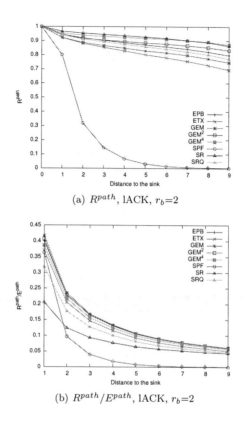

(a) R^{path}, lACK, $r_b=2$

(b) R^{path}/E^{path}, lACK, $r_b=2$

Figure 3.18: Simulation Results: R^{path} and R^{path}/E^{path} in the lazy acknowledgement scheme

ward path transport reliability, considerably outperforms the other metrics and achieves the record sensor network lifetime of 500 rounds. Additionally, *SR* achieves the highest R^{path} values compared to other metrics (see Fig. 3.18a)) and provides the second worst value of energy efficiency as plotted in Fig. 3.18b) after the *SPF* metric. The reason for these results of *SR* combined with the lazy acknowledgement scheme lies in the distribution of energy consumption between a child node and its parent in the routing tree. For implicit and explicit acknowledgement schemes, besides forwarding

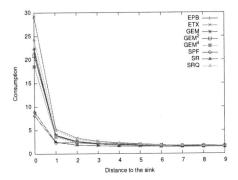

Figure 3.19: Simulation Results: Distribution of the energy consumption between the child and the parent node in the lazy acknowledgement scheme (1ACK, $r_b=2$)

packets from its children, the parent node additionally has to acknowledge each packet successfully received. This causes a considerable energy consumption on the parent node even if λ is small. The lazy acknowledgement scheme considerably relieves the parent node, as a successful packet delivery does not require any additional effort of the parent node. Therefore, routing metrics that tend to select links with a high forward link quality save energy on the parent nodes. This is the optimization goal of the *SR* metric (see Fig. 3.19b) for the average values of energy consumption of sensor nodes based on their relative distance to the sink).

Finally, the first nodes that run out of energy in our grid topology are located around the sink node. Therefore, saving energy of the parent nodes along the routing path, which is achieved due to combining the *SR* metric with the lazy acknowledgement scheme, considerably prolongs the lifetime of the sensor network.

Other energy-aware routing metrics optimize the *overall* path energy regardless of the distribution of load between a child and its parent and, therefore, lead to worse results. *GEM*^{x} approaches *SR* for $x \to \infty$.

3.8 Structure Analysis

In this section, we summarize the properties of the discussed routing metrics and several other popular routing protocols with respect to the routing structures they construct. The results of our analysis are summarized in Table 3.3.

In Section 2.4, we discussed the importance of the stability, reconfiguration and convergence properties of structuring algorithms. Stability and reconfiguration are mutually conflicting properties. Highly stable structures are badly reconfigurable and a high reconfigurability usually leads to an overly sensitive system and, thus, to instability and a permanent reconfiguration overhead. Therefore, we say that a structure has a good stability and is easily reconfigurable if both characteristics are well balanced.

Stability, reconfigurability and convergence are highly relevant for algorithms targeted at constructing efficient routing trees. We have shown in Section 3.7 that the *SPF* routing metric surprisingly leads to the construction of a stable structure due to the smoothing nature of a link quality estimator based on a moving average and the fact that only the existence of a link and not its quality is considered. The other discussed routing metrics, *ETX*, *EPB* and *GEM*, provide good results on tree stability and reconfigurability because they utilize link estimations in a non-linear fashion. Thus, a substantial noise margin should be used in the parent selection to increase the stability [WTC03]. However, the optimization of the network transport reliability done by *SR* severely degrades the tree stability as it is very sensitive to the fluctuation of the link estimation. However, a routing protocol based on any routing metric discussed in this thesis can be stabilized by introducing a threshold value and thus limiting the fluctuation of the estimated link qualities.

Routing protocols based on any of the discussed routing metrics are quickly reconfigurable if the network topology changes due to node failures or the environment. Moreover, routing metric-based protocols quickly converge to a tree structure.

Every structuring algorithm generates construction and maintenance overhead. The algorithms generating global structures usually lead to a high overhead which degrades the reconfigurability of the structures and the scalability of the algorithm, even in the case where the structure itself can be considered scalable.

Despite being a global structure, a routing tree is a scalable structure because it is hierarchical and *self-similar*, i.e. the structure looks similar for any node

Property	GEM^x	SPF	ETX/ EPB/SR	Flooding	Geogr. Routing
Stab./Reconfig.	+	+	+	-	+
Convergence	+	+	+	N/A	+
Param./Adapt.	+	-	-	-	-
Temp./Static	S	S	S	-	S/T
Coordinates	-	-	-	-	+
Mobility	-	-	-	+	-/+
Scalability	+	+	+	-	+
Overhead	high	high	high	none	high
TopDown/BottomUp	TD	TD	TD	-	BU

Table 3.3: Classification of routing algorithms and obtained structures

in the network. Every node (except the sink) has a parent and can have several children. All routing protocols based on routing metrics exploit this property of the tree structure. However, the overhead of the construction and maintenance of a tree structure is not negligible. Firstly, the link estimator has to monitor the state of multiple links to neighbor nodes. Secondly, the routing metric has to propagate accumulated values of path characteristics through the network.

We have compared the routing metric-based routing protocols with two other popular routing approaches: *Geographic routing* and *Flooding*.

Geographic routing [KGKS06] (e.g., *GPSR* [KK00]) is a class of routing approaches that leverage the knowledge of node coordinates in a global co-ordinate system for the forwarding of messages. *Geographic routing* applies greedy forwarding whenever possible. This means that packets are always forwarded to the neighboring node with the smallest distance to the desti-nation coordinate. When a packet reaches a region where greedy forwarding is impossible, the algorithm recovers by routing along the perimeter of the region. Greedy forwarding requires that every node possesses position in-formation of its immediate neighbors in the network connectivity graph. Perimeter forwarding requires prior planarization of a network graph which is quite expensive [KGKS06]. There are existing heuristics that minimize the overhead in the common case but cannot reduce the general complexity.

We have included the *Flooding* protocol to our selection of routing protocols. This protocol does not build any structure: data messages are always flooded to all the nodes in the network. Thus, every message eventually reaches the sink node. *Flooding* does not generate any structure construction or maintenance overhead. However, as every message is forwarded to every node in the network, *Flooding* exhibits very poor scalability.

All routing protocols except *Flooding* and *Geographic Routing* do not handle node mobility very well. Moreover, routing trees are rarely constructed temporarily. *Flooding* is the only protocol that is able to work in highly mobile environments because it does not construct any structure and takes advantage of the broadcast medium.

Due to the high cost of reliable perimeter forwarding, *Geographic routing* generates a high reconfiguration overhead and does not support node mobility well. Again, heuristic planarization approaches help to cope with limited mobility in most cases.

Algorithms can construct structures in a top-down or bottom-up manner. The way the algorithm constructs the structure can heavily influence the cost of its reconfiguration, its scalability, the maintenance overhead and its mobility support. Routing trees are constructed with the help of routing metrics by building paths starting from the sink down to every sensor node. Knowledge of node coordinates allows *Geographic Routing* approaches to construct paths from every node to the sink in a bottom-up manner. In this case, a bottom-up solution requires solving the graph planarization problem in order to perform perimeter routing.

The ability of structuring algorithms to be parameterized is important for adapting the structure to different application requirements or specific target environments. Routing tree structures optimized for transport reliability look very different from structures optimized for energy efficiency. Moreover, the properties of the target environment are difficult to predict before the deployment. Parameterized algorithms allow tuning the structure and adjusting its properties instead of reprogramming nodes. An example of a parameterized routing metric is GEM^x, which is one of the main contributions of this work.

3.9 Summary

In this chapter, we have investigated the problem of constructing an energy-efficient routing metric. We have provided a definition of energy efficiency with respect to routing metrics which is missing in prior work. An analysis of energy-efficiency as an optimization goal for routing metrics has shown its inherent non-optimality for routing trees.

We have proposed an accurate modeling of the link layer acknowledgement scheme and of the expected transport reliability and the energy consumption of a path. This model considers the maximum number of retransmissions to be limited, and therefore, we especially take into account the acceptance of packet losses as an important distinguishing characteristic of wireless sensor networks. Based on this model, we have proposed the new energy-efficient routing metric GEM^x. Since this metric considers different acknowledgement schemes, asymmetric links and the variable number of retransmissions and transmission power level, it is applicable to a wide range of scenarios. Additionally, compared to other existing energy-efficient metrics, it provides the unique possibility to shift the emphasis between a higher transport reliability and a lower energy consumption in order to adapt to specific requirements.

We have discussed existing metrics proposed for energy-efficiency in wireless sensor networks: *ETX*, *EPB*, *SR* and *SRQ*. We have shown the weaknesses and simplifications of the respective models and have constructed improved versions of these metrics. Additionally, we have shown that GEM^x encompasses most metrics as special cases, e.g., by assuming that the maximum number of retransmissions is unlimited.

The evaluation has shown that GEM^x outperforms existing metrics with regard to energy efficiency despite the inherent non-optimality of energy-efficiency as an optimization goal for routing trees. We have shown the behavior resulting from tuning x and discussed the relations to the other metrics as special cases of GEM^x.

In addition to empirical results, we have provided a theoretical analysis of energy-efficient routing metrics with respect to the important properties loop-freeness, optimality and consistency. We have also shown the incompleteness of the conditions for being consistent, optimal and loop-free presented by [YW08] for dynamic networks and provided a corrected version of it for these scenarios. Additionally, we have discussed the sensitivity to changes of node parameters – the transmission power level and the maximum number of transmissions – and the behavior of GEM^x and existing metrics with respect to their individual optimization goals.

We have analyzed the properties of a tree structure constructed by the discussed routing metrics and have compared it to the results of other routing paradigms. This analysis revealed the group of sensor network applications that benefits from constructing and maintaining routing trees.

3.10 Appendix: Terminology

$G(V, E)$	Directed graph that models a sensor network
V	Set of nodes
E	Set of communication links
node 0	Base station or a sink node
$p \in (0, 1]$	Forward connectivity of a given link
$q \in (0, 1]$	Backward connectivity of a given link
(p, q)	Link connectivity or link quality
$e_f \in \mathbb{R}^+$	Energy cost of a forward link
$e_b \in \mathbb{R}^+$	Energy cost of a backward link
(e_f, e_b)	Link cost
$\lambda = \frac{e_b}{e_f}$	Constant used to calculate per bit characteristics
l	Transmission power level (TPL) of a given node
$\mathbb{L}$	Set of available TPLs
$e : \mathbb{L} \to \mathbb{R}^+ \times \mathbb{R}^+$	Mapping of a TPL l to the link cost (e_f, e_b)
$i \in V$	A sensor node
$\langle i, i - 1 \rangle$	Directed link from node i to node $i - 1$ in a path
E_{init}^i	Initial amount of energy of node i
$d = n..0$	Path from node n to the sink 0
T_G	Routing tree
$(W, \preceq, L, \Sigma, \phi, \oplus, f)$	Algebra representation of a routing metric
L	Set of labels corresponding to links
Σ	Set of signatures
$\oplus$	Path append operation
ϕ	Signature that indicates the absence of a path
W	Set of weights
f	Mapping of signatures to weights
$\preceq$	Total order over weights
r_f	Number of transmissions along forward link
r_b	Number of transmissions along backward link
$R_{r_f}^{link}$	Link transport reliability
$E_{r_f}^{link}$	Link energy consumption
$R_{r_f}^{path}$	Path transport reliability
$E_{r_f}^{path}$	Path energy consumption
x	Tuning parameter of GEM^x routing metric

4 ST-Grouping

This chapter present an algorithm for constructing groups of sensor nodes to enable sensing of composite events. Most works on sensing in wireless sensor networks use only very simple sensors, e.g. humidity or temperature, to illustrate their concepts. However, in a large number of scenarios including structural health monitoring, more complex sensors that usually employ medium to high frequency sampling and post-processing are required. Additionally, to capture an event completely several sensors of different types are needed which have to be in range of the event and used in a timely manner. In this chapter, we study the problem of space-bounded and time-bounded grouping (*ST-Grouping*) where the parallel use of different sensors on the same node is impossible and not all nodes possess all required sensors. We provide a model formalizing the requirements and present algorithms for spatial grouping and temporal scheduling to tackle these problems.

4.1 Preliminaries

Although it is often theoretically possible to equip the sensor nodes with all required complex sensors, this might cause several problems. First, each additional complex sensor requires energy, which degrades the lifetime of the individual sensor node and of the whole network. Second, it is often difficult or impossible to trigger and sample several complex sensors at the same time. Moreover, the triggers of two separate sensors activated by an event will not happen simultaneously, which makes simultaneous sampling quite complex. Third, each sensor has its own area of regard. Therefore, some sensors might register abnormality of one environmental characteristic when capturing events, with no confirmation from other attached sensors with a smaller sensing range. Fourth, attaching all sensors to every sensor node still requires much cable to place the sensors at meaningful locations. For example in bridge monitoring scenario, an acceleration sensor used to measure cable forces must be attached to the corresponding cable whereas an acoustic sensor must be embedded into the bridge floor to be able to acquire acoustic waves which might indicate cracks in the construction. Therefore, in many cases there is a strong need for the distribution of sensors among several sensor nodes and for further in-network cooperation of space-bounded sensors and grouping of time-bounded sensor values in order to detect and characterize an event. Fifth, sensing takes time and for highly dynamic events, like the occurrence of a crack in a bridge, it is impossible to inquire several sensors sequentially within the event duration.

In this chapter we assume that every sensor node has one or several sensors attached. These sensors try to capture events that can only be detected within a limited range in space and within a limited period in time. On the one hand, we present algorithms that establish space-bounded non-disjoint groups of sensor nodes which can be seen as one logical sensor node for recognizing an event. On the other hand, we present a scheduling algorithm that allows the distribution of sensing tasks in every group and creates a local task schedule for every sensor on every individual sensor node.

Our approach can be used to achieve two goals: to recognize events that activate hardware triggers or to answer pre-distributed user queries. In the first case, on the fly space-bounded group establishment and fast time-bounded scheduling algorithms are required. This is also needed if some sensor nodes are mobile. In the second case, groups and schedules can be established as soon as the query is received.

Our approach requires neither global knowledge of the sensor network topology or resource distribution nor sensor node coordinates. We can calculate the vicinity based on local communication graphs. The received signal strength indicator (RSSI) and node coordinates are used if available in order to improve the results.

4.2 Related Work

Several topics are related to our approach including event detection and query execution, spatial node grouping or clustering and distributed job scheduling. In this section we discuss prior papers in these fields and their relations to this work.

Event detection is a popular research area in WSN [VBL07, OAVRH06, RM04b, MSS97]. The event detection system presented in [JKV05] allows the detection of composite events in case nodes have heterogeneous sensing capabilities. The results described in [VBL07, OAVRH06, KI04] provide algorithms for the detection of k-watched composite events, where each event occurrence can be detected by at least k sensors. In [RM04b], the authors concentrate on state transitions of the environment rather than on states only and discuss a generalized view on event detection in WSNs. They model state transitions with finite automata. However, this model is impractical due to its complexity. The authors of [MSS97] consider the problem of describing events or states and state transitions of the environment with an event description language. The main difference of the mentioned works to our approach is that only the spatial characteristic of event detection has been considered. Since an event happens at some point in space and *time*, we also consider its temporal characteristic. Moreover, most papers in this group consider spatial node grouping to increase the confidence of the sensing results. In this work we group nodes in order to be able to process complex queries and detect complex events.

A number of research projects including TinyDB [MFHH05] and Cougar [FSG02] have considered a query-based database abstraction of the WSN. However, these works assume that the sensor nodes possess the same unordered set of sensors and that the actual access of these sensors is not time limited. Therefore, the sequential execution of the sensing tasks that compose the query on every node is always possible. In this chapter we motivate and provide a solution for the case when sequential execution of sensing tasks on every node is impossible.

There are a number of papers that consider the problem of spatial node grouping or clustering [YS07, HHT02] in WSN. The usual reason for this grouping is to allow for efficient data aggregation in sensor networks and, therefore, save energy of individual nodes. In this work we present node grouping algorithms that try to construct the maximum number of complete groups – groups that have all required sensing capabilities to fulfil the query (or detect an event) and thus can play the role of one logical sensor node.

Another related group of approaches includes role distribution algorithms [FR05]. Our work differs from traditional role distribution approaches because roles assigned inside of one logical group are defined by the set of sensors every node contributes to the group.

The problem of job scheduling is closely related to our work. This problem is usually formulated as follows: Given a directed acyclic graph, where vertices represent jobs and an edge (u, v) indicates that task u must be completed before task v. The goal is to find a schedule of tasks which requires the minimum amount of time or machines. Additional resource constraints on every machine and resource requirements for every task may exist. There are also a number of solutions to this problem in different formulations [Bru07]. However, in this work we also consider concurrency constraints between tasks, which reduces the applicability of existing solutions to our problem. Therefore, we present a new scheduling algorithm for sensor networks which allows the scheduling of sensing tasks between different sensor nodes taking concurrency constraints between individual tasks into account.

4.3 ST-Grouping

In this section we first motivate the need for *ST-Grouping* based on the example taken from the structural health monitoring application. Then, we present the terminology and assumptions used throughout this work and describe the problem of space-bounded and time-bounded grouping in these terms.

4.3.1 Application Example: Structural Monitoring

One of the most promising examples of real-world applications of WSNs is the structural monitoring of bridges [NOM, MBSF06, KPC$^+$06], tunnels [KKK$^+$06] or buildings [XRC$^+$04]. Such monitoring systems are usually focused at long-time (up to few years) monitoring of large and important structures and are used to replace traditional high-cost cable-based monitoring systems or periodic inspections. Typical sensors for this application include:

- *acoustic sensors* which can detect cracks or breaks in a concrete structure by sensing an acoustic signal (triggered, sampling rate: ~40-100kHz, duration of sampling: 5-40ms);

- *acceleration sensor* for the calculation of natural frequencies (sampling rate: ~100-200Hz, duration of sampling: 10 × 0.5-1s);

- *strain gauges* provide a highly localized indication of stress concentration or strain behavior at critical locations (sampling rate: ~0-50Hz, duration of sampling: 1-2s);

- *vibration sensor* for calculation of ambient vibrations (sampling rate: ~1kHz, duration of sampling: 1ms);

- *temperature and humidity sensors* influence the crack detection algorithms (sampling rate: once per 10 minutes, duration of sampling: 220ms and 75ms respectively).

As motivated above, it is quite difficult and energy-inefficient to equip one sensor node with all sensors or alternatively send all complex information to the base station for combination. Therefore, in-network data processing and event detection are of great importance to prolong the lifetime of a sensor network. To enable cooperation, we present space-bounded node grouping and time-bounded scheduling of sensing tasks. But first we have to introduce some terminology, several assumptions and a formal definition of the problem.

4.3.2 Terminology, Assumptions and Problem Statement

Let us start by introducing the terminology used in this chapter (summarized in a table in Section 4.8). We model the *sensor network* as an *undirected graph* $G(V, E)$ embedded into the plane, where V is a set of nodes and E is the set of edges between nodes that can communicate. Every node $v_i \in V$ in this *embedding* $p : V \to \mathbb{R}^2$ has coordinates $(x_i, y_i) \in \mathbb{R}^2$ on the plane. However, as explained later, it is not necessary for our approach that the nodes are aware of their coordinates. We consider that all sensor nodes are embedded within some *target area* $A \subset \mathbb{R}^2$ on the plane. Additionally, the function $v : V \to 2^{\mathbb{S}}$ defines the sensor types each node possesses where $\mathbb{S}$ is the domain of sensor types used in the scenario. This implies that each node contains at most one sensor of each type.

A *query* or *event description* $Q = (S, R, D, C, Pred)$ is defined as a 5-tuple. The set $S \subseteq \mathbb{S}$ describes the sensor types used in the query. The functions $R : S \to \mathbb{R}$ and $D : S \to \mathbb{D}$ describe the sensing range and sensing time respectively for each sensor type in S. We assume a sensing area to be a disc with radius $r \in \mathbb{R}$. The sensing time only describes the actual time needed to access the sensor readings. This duration does not include any data processing, filtering or aggregation actions which can be arbitrarily postponed. Additionally, the concurrency constraints between different sensor types are captured by $C : S \times S \to \mathbb{R}$. For each pair of sensor types, an element of C defines the maximum duration between starting the sensing of the corresponding sensors. *Pred* is a predicate which maps the sensor values of each sensor type and the combination of these values to {true,false}. We do not further discuss possible definitions of this predicate since we do not extend the large amount of prior work regarding this topic. The combination of these characteristics is extremely important because, for example, a break in a concrete structure event can be captured by an acoustic sensor only within several microseconds in a range of several meters, whereas a fire event results in a temperature increase that can be measured by a temperature sensor within several minutes within a range dependent on the fire event itself (centimetres for a fire of a candle till hundreds of meters for a fire in a forest). We refer to the sensing duration and concurrency constraints and to the sensing range of a query or event description as *event time and space* constraints.

The sensing range of an event with respect to a specific sensor coincides with a sensing range the sensor has and depends on the sensitivity of the sensor. The event duration is, however, usually longer than the sensing duration of the sensor. For example, an acoustic event results in a series of acoustic emissions or fire event lasts longer than needed by a temperature sensor to read the value. The event duration as well as the additional dependencies between the sensing with different sensor types have to be captured by the concurrency constraints. The support for concurrency constraints is also a main difference to related approaches, where usually parallel sensing of all sensors is considered.

Our main assumption is that if an event happens at some location $P \in \mathbb{R}^2$ and at some point in time $T_0 \in \mathbb{R}$ and is sensed by a group of sensors which comprises all required sensor types S and satisfies time and space constraints D, C, R with respect to the starting point of the event in time and the point in space respectively, then the sensor readings obtained are a good approximation of the event characteristics. This assumption is very natural for sensor networks.

We define a group of sensors $G_i \subseteq S \times V$, if $\forall (s_j, v_k^i) \in G_i, s_j \in v(v_k^i)$ and $\forall s_j \in S, \exists (s_j, v_k^i) \in G_i$. This ensures, that only sensor types of a node are used if this node actually possesses the type and that all sensor types required by the query are contained at least once in the group. Let dist denote the Euclidean distance, we say that a group G_i is space-bounded with respect to a certain event, if $\forall (s_j, v_k^i) \in G_i, \text{dist}(P, p(v_k^i)) \leq R(s_j)$. This requires that all sensors of each type are in range of the event. However, the definition of a group does not require that for every node all sensor types it possesses are used in the group. This allows the creation of groups where for some nodes only the long-range sensors (e.g. temperature) are used and the short range sensors are ignored. The missing sensor types have to be supplied by nodes closer to the event.

We assume, that parallel sampling of two sensors on the same sensor node is impossible. Two sensors can be accessed sequentially only. Every sensor s_j has its sensing duration $D(s_j)$ – the time the sensor node requires to obtain the sensor readings from this sensor.

We refer to a local schedule J_i^{local} for a sensor node v_i as a sequence of sensing tasks that need to be executed for the complete or a fraction of an event description Q. The schedule contains the start times for the access of every sensor type. As described above, the sensing tasks may not overlap; however, it is possible to insert idle times between two sensing tasks. A local schedule is *time-bounded* if the sequence of sensing tasks fulfils the concurrency constraints C.

A *group schedule* J_i for a group G_i is defined correspondingly to the local schedule but includes information for all sensing tasks of all group members. A group schedule is time-bounded if the local schedules it includes are time-bounded and additionally the concurrency constraints C between sensor types on different nodes are met, which can require the inclusion of idle times on individual nodes.

The problem of time-bounded and space-bounded grouping (*ST-Grouping*) is:

> *Define a group of nodes and a schedule that enable the execution of the query Q under the given time, concurrency and space constraints.*

In the following subsections we consider the problem of time-bounded and space-bounded grouping separately as well as in combination with distributed coordination.

4.3.3 Time-Bounded Sensing

Consider the case when an individual sensor node is equipped with all required sensors to process the query Q. It is easy to construct a schedule that sequentially fetches sensor readings from each of these sensors in order to evaluate Q and send the aggregated result to the data sink. Here a simple algorithm can be used to try every possible permutation in order to find a schedule that fulfils the concurrency constraints. Since the number of sensors on a node is usually quite low (≤ 5), it is easy even on resource constrained sensor network devices to enumerate all possible permutations.

As discussed below, additional concurrency dependencies between the individual nodes must also be satisfied when distributing sensing tasks including the distribution delays. We model the scheduling problem as a graph in which the vertices represent sensing tasks with their corresponding task durations and the edges represent the concurrency constraints between each pair of tasks. As an example, in Fig. 4.1 it is required to execute a query or detect an event with sensors $\{s_1, s_2, s_3, s_4\}$ to obtain an aggregated result of the 4 sensors. The problem is to schedule the sensing tasks $s_1 - s_4$ with task durations $3, 2, 2, 2$ respectively. The concurrency constraints express the maximum difference in time between the start times of each pair of tasks. In the example, the presented two sensor nodes can combine their efforts to fulfil this query.

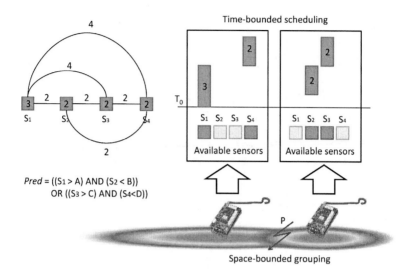

Figure 4.1: Motivating example for *ST-Grouping*: Resource conflicts in time and space

We define the duration $\mathrm{Dur}(J)$ of a schedule as the time from starting to sense the first task to the completion of the last task. Additionally, we define a general metric $\varphi(J)$ indicating the badness of a schedule. We use a badness metric instead of a quality metric since for most intuitive approaches, e.g. the duration of a schedule, higher values mean worse results. This is also consistent to the dispersion metric used for space-bounded sensing described below. Using this metric, we describe the challenge of time-bounded sensing as an optimization problem:

$$\varphi(J_i) \rightarrow \mathbf{min}$$
$$J_i \text{ is a valid schedule as defined above} \tag{4.1}$$

In particular, J_i must fulfil the concurrency constraints between the execution start times of different tasks. Note that classical scheduling algorithms from the literature do not assume any concurrency dependencies between the tasks.

4.3.4 Space-Bounded Sensing

If an individual sensor node does not possess all required sensors to fulfil the query or check the event description, popular approaches, e.g. TinyDB [MFHH05], fail to consider this node. However, it might be possible to combine two nodes, each with an incomplete set of sensors, located close to each other. From the viewpoint of the application, a space-bounded group plays the role of *one logical sensor node* which possesses all sensors that the group has and allows to perform operations over such space-bounded sensor readings, e.g. calculate if the sensor readings confirm to a certain event description. Prior work in this field [JKV05,VBL07,OAVRH06,KI04] focuses on the combination of the nodes within a sensing range of an event. In this thesis we additionally consider the space inaccuracy of such combination and try to reduce it.

Since the location of an event is not known, we instead introduce a dispersion metric $\psi : S \times V \to \mathbb{R}$. Our approach can work with different metrics. Besides metrics based on actual node coordinates, e.g. the maximum distance from the centroid of the group, metrics based only on some proximity information such as RSSI or the number of shared neighbors are possible. Therefore, we formulate the optimization problem of space-bounded sensing as follows:

$$\psi(G_i) \to \mathbf{min}$$
$$G_i \text{ is a valid group as defined above} \tag{4.2}$$

4.3.5 Distributed Coordination

The formulated time-bounded and space-bounded sensing problems consider time and space as limited resources in the context of event detection or phenomena monitoring.

Consider the case when all nodes are equipped with a complete set of sensors. A *time resource conflict* occurs, when it is impossible to acquire an event with a single sensor node via sequential scheduling of sensing tasks due to concurrency constraints. This problem can be solved by intelligent relocation of a fraction of the local schedule to the nodes close-by.

A *spatial resource conflict* occurs if a node does not possess the required set of sensors to process the query. In this case, the event must be captured by in-network cooperation of a group of sensor nodes. If the sequential scheduling on every individual node does not result in any problems, the solution

		Time	
		No resource conflict	Resource conflict
Space	**No resource conflict**	Situation: • Sensor node is equipped with all needed sensors; • Sequential sensing is possible; Approach: • One node; • Sequential sensing;	Situation: • It is possible to path a fraction of sensing sequence to space-related neighbors; • Sequential sensing is NOT possible within event duration; Approach: • Several nodes; • Parallel sensing; • Distributed time coordination;
	Resource conflict	Situation: • The sensor node is NOT equipped with all needed sensors; • Sequential sensing is possible; Approach: • Several nodes; • Parallel or sequential sensing; • Distributed space coordination;	Situation: • The sensor node is NOT equipped with all needed sensors; • Sequential sensing is NOT possible within event duration; Approach: • Several nodes; • Parallel sensing; • Distributed spatial-temporal coordination;

Figure 4.2: Problem space of time-bounded and space-bounded grouping

involves group coordination mechanism which partitions the sensor network in space-bounded groups equipped with all required sensors to process the query. Then every group operates as a single logical sensor node.

In real world deployments both problems might occur. In this case, the distribution of sensing tasks in space by space-bounded group coordination and intelligent distributed scheduling of sensing tasks is the only possible solution. Fig. 4.2 summarizes the described problem space.

4.4 Algorithms

After describing the model for time-bounded and space-bounded sensing, we now discuss the algorithms we have developed first to construct groups of nodes containing all required sensors and then to compute a schedule to fulfil the requirements.

4.4.1 Ordering of Sensors

As described in the problem statement, both algorithms have to solve an optimization problem. The problem of constructing a local schedule when all sensor types are available on a node is quite easy – simply enumerating all possible permutations yields the desired result. However, the problem of finding a set of nodes to form a complete group or to generate a valid group schedule spanning several nodes is a much harder problem. Therefore, we introduce a total order among sensor types to greatly reduce the complexity of the algorithms. This order does not pose any unduly restrictions for the query definition, since the priorities can often be derived quite naturally from the characteristics of the employed sensor types. For example, humidity and temperature sensors are not very time sensitive and can be sampled with low priority and are thus among the last of the order. Very complex sensors, e.g. acoustic emission sensors, that may even rely on hardware triggers and thus initiate the complete event detection process, should be placed first in the order.

To express the total order, we redefine a query for our algorithms in terms of vectors and matrices. A query $\tilde{Q} = (\vec{S}, \vec{R}, \vec{D}, C, \textit{Pred})$ on n sensor types comprises the sensor types $\vec{S} = (s_1, \ldots, s_n), s_i \in \mathbb{S}$, the associated sensing ranges $\vec{R} = (r_1, \ldots, r_n), r_i \in \mathbb{R}$ and sensing durations $\vec{D} = (d_1, \ldots, d_n), d_i \in \mathbb{R}$ as well as a symmetric $n \times n$ matrix C where each element $c_{ij} \in \mathbb{R}$ defines the maximum duration between the start times of sensor type i and sensor type j. As described above, the definition of the predicate $\textit{Pred}$ is beyond the scope of our algorithm.

Additionally, we reduce the number of allowed sensors of the same type in a group to one. Therefore, a group $\vec{G} = (v_1, \ldots, v_n), v_i \in V$ simply indicates for each sensor type the corresponding node. Accordingly, a schedule $\vec{J} = (t_1, \ldots, t_n), t_i \in \mathbb{R}$ defines the start times of each sensor type. Of course a valid schedule still has to fulfil all concurrency constraints and guarantee the sequential execution of sensing tasks on each individual node.

4.4.2 Space-Bounded Group Establishment

As stated above, the goal of space-bounded group establishment is to build *tight* groups, where tight is defined in terms of a dispersion metric ψ : $S \times V \to \mathbb{R}$. We distinguish between three parts of our algorithm, which we describe in detail below. For each part, we have developed two alternatives. Since all combinations are possible, we have evaluated eight different algorithm combinations.

For each group, one node is distinguished as the leader of the group (comparable to a cluster head). This is always the node of which the first sensor type is used. The groups are built iteratively on the basis of the order of sensor types. At initialization, all nodes that possess the first sensor start forming groups by looking for nodes with the second sensor type. Which nodes are available for addition to a group is determined by the *selection rule*. Of course only nodes which have the correct sensor type are considered. The best node is then selected based on the *dispersion metric*. This step is performed for the following sensor types until the group is complete or as long as a suitable node is found. Each sensor of each node can only be used in one group. We now describe each step in more detail and show the implementations we used.

Dispersion metric

The dispersion metric was already defined in 4.3.4. The dispersion metric has to be computed at each step (for the selection of each sensor type) and with each candidate node. Let $\vec{G}_p$ denote a partially complete group consisting of the already selected sensor types and a candidate node for the sensor type that is currently required. Let $k = |\vec{G}_p|$ denote the number of sensor types in this partial group. Then $\text{centroid}(\vec{G}_p) = (\frac{1}{k} \sum_{v_i \in \vec{G}_p} x_i, \frac{1}{k} \sum_{v_i \in \vec{G}_p} y_i)$ defines the centroid of the partial group. Note that if multiple sensors of one node are used in the group, this results in a higher weighting factor for that node. We define the standard deviation $SDev = (\frac{1}{k} \sum_{v_i \in \vec{G}_p} dist(p(v_i), \text{centroid}_x(\vec{G}_p))^2)^{\frac{1}{2}}$ and the maximum of the distances to the centroid $Rad = \max_{v_i \in \vec{G}_p} dist(p(v_i), \text{centroid}_x(\vec{G}_p))$ as our two metrics. Both metrics require node coordinates, however, as already described above this is not a general requirement for our approach.

Selection rule

The selection rule defines which nodes to consider for the next sensor type. We define the *Group* selection rule where all neighbors of all group members (in addition to the current group members itself) are considered. The *Leader* selection rule allows only the neighbors of the leader of a group (besides itself) to be added. These rules differ obviously in communication cost, since the collection of candidates as well as the actual selection requires message transmissions. Therefore, the *Group* selection rule allows choosing from a larger number of candidates at the expense of increased communication costs. We detail the different performances in the evaluation section.

Grouping algorithm

The grouping algorithm defines the overall process of group building. We implemented a rather simple *FirstChoice* algorithm. A leader simply selects the next node based on the selection rule and the dispersion metric. The first leader that chooses the sensor on another node wins. Our second approach *BestChoice* is more complicated. A leader informs a selected node not only with its ID but also with the value of the dispersion metric, which the new node saves. If another leader later selects the same sensor on the same node and the dispersion metric of this group is better than the saved one, the node changes the group and informs the former leader about its decision. The former leader then discards all selected sensors of a lower priority and begins rebuilding its group. This algorithm is detailed in Fig. 4.3. However, since this algorithm involves backtracking, we have to show that it converges.

Lemma 4.4.1. *The BestChoice algorithm converges if the dispersion metric has a lower bound.*

Proof. Consider the process of constructing one separate spatial group by the *BestChoice* algorithm. We prove the statement by induction on the number of sensors in the group. Base of induction: If the group must contain only one sensor, the algorithm converges. Induction step: consider the algorithm converges for k nodes in the group. The next node is determined by requesting the ungrouped node (equipped with the needed sensor) which minimizes the values of the dispersion metric to join the group. However, the node might reject joining the group for another group with a smaller value of the dispersion metric. This process iterates until the node joins the best group among all offers and the group chooses the best node from all ungrouped nodes. Since the value of the dispersion metric is minimized at each step, the existence of the lower bound guarantees that the algorithm terminates. The transitivity of the min relation ensures that the final state does not contain deadlocks. □

Procedure `bestChoice`

---

for $j = 2$ **to** n **do**
  | $\text{leader}_j \leftarrow \inf$
  | $\text{leaderMetric}_j \leftarrow \inf$
endfor
if *isLeader* **then**
  | `search(`*1*`)`
endif

Procedure `search(`*sensor*`)`

$(v_{\text{cand}}, \text{metric}) \leftarrow \text{findCand}(\text{sensor}, G_i, V_{\text{ignore}}^{\text{sensor}})$
if *metric* > 0 **then**
  | `send(`v_{cand}`, `*SELECT, sensor, metric*`)`
endif

Procedure `onReceive(`*what, sender, sensor*`)`

---

if *what* $= ACCEPT$ **then**
  | $G_k \leftarrow \text{sender}$
  | **if** *sensor* $< n$ **then**
    | `search(`*sensor+1*`)`
  | **endif**
endif
if *what* $= REJECT$ **then**
  | $V_{\text{ignore}}^{\text{sensor}} \leftarrow V_{\text{ignore}}^{\text{sensor}} \cup \{v_{\text{sender}}\}$
  | `search(`*sensor*`)`
endif
if *what* $= SELECT$ **then**
  | **if** *leaderMetric$_{sensor}$* $>$ *metric* **then**
    | **if** *leader$_{sensor}$* $\neq \inf$ **then**
      | `send(`*leader$_{sensor}$, REJECT, sensor*`)`
    | **endif**
    | $\text{leaderMetric}_{\text{sensor}} \leftarrow \text{metric}$
    | $\text{leader}_{\text{sensor}} \leftarrow \text{sender}$
    | `send(`*sender, ACCEPT, sensor*`)`
  | **else**
    | `send(`*sender, REJECT, sensor*`)`
  | **endif**
endif

Figure 4.3: The BestChoice algorithm

Procedure `schedule`

`/* returns start times` $\vec{t}$ `of all sensor tasks` `*/`

$\vec{t} \leftarrow \vec{0}$

$\text{minStart} \leftarrow 0$

$\text{current} \leftarrow 2$

for $1 = 1$ **to** n **do**
| $\text{nodeBusy}_{\vec{G}_i} \leftarrow 0$
endfor

$\text{nodeBusy}_{\vec{G}_1} \leftarrow d_1$

while $current \leq n$ **do**
| $\text{minTime} \leftarrow \max(\text{nodeBusy}_{\vec{G}_{current}}, minStart)$
| $\text{good} \leftarrow \textbf{TRUE}$
| **for** $i = current\text{-}1$ **to** n **step** -1 **do**
| | $\text{minTime} \leftarrow \max(minTime, t_i - C_{currenti}))$
| | **if** $minTime > t_i - C_{currenti}$ **then**
| | | **if** $i = 1$ **then**   `// impossible`
| | | | **return** $-\vec{1}$
| | | **endif**
| | | $\text{minStart} \leftarrow \text{minTime} -C_{\text{current}i}$
| | | $\text{nodeBusy} \leftarrow \vec{0}$
| | | **for** $j \leftarrow 1 \ldots i - 1$ **do**
| | | | $\text{nodeBusy}_{\vec{G}_j} \leftarrow t_j + d_j$
| | | **endfor**
| | | $\text{current} \leftarrow i$
| | | $\text{good} \leftarrow \textbf{FALSE}$
| | | **break**
| | **endif**
| **endfor**
| **if** *good* **then**
| | $t_{\text{current}} \leftarrow \text{minTime}$
| | $\text{nodeBusy}_{\vec{G}_{\text{current}}} \leftarrow \text{minTime} + d_{\text{current}}$
| | $\text{current} \leftarrow \text{current+1}$
| | $\text{minStart} \leftarrow 0$
| **endif**
endw

return $\vec{t}$

Figure 4.4: The scheduling algorithm

4.4.3 Time-Bounded Scheduling

We have developed an algorithm that generates a group schedule fulfilling the concurrency constraints and minimizing the duration $\text{Dur}(J)$ of the whole schedule. The total order of sensor types allows a very efficient non-recursive algorithm, which is detailed in Fig. 4.4. The algorithm is based on backtracking. However, due to the priorities, the start time of a task may only monotonically increase, which limits the number of backtrackings. The algorithm always finds the schedule with the minimal duration. As a slight simplification, we do not include the time that is necessary to notify all members of the group. However, this interval can simply be inserted at the beginning of the local schedules. The problem of inter-group conflicts when an event can be sensed by several groups and the sensors of one node are used in different groups is left for future work. However, priorities provide a deterministic method to select which sensor on a node is used first in case of a conflict.

4.5 Evaluation

The evaluation of our approach is based on thorough simulations with different node densities, different numbers of sensor types required to detect an event or process the query and two settings of concurrency constraints. The sensor nodes are distributed in an area of $900 \times 530 \text{ m}^2$. In all figures we distributed between 150 and 450 sensor nodes in the area which results in average node degrees between 9 and 26. We constructed topologies using perturbed grids to create the scenarios: the nodes are placed randomly inside of circles arranged in a regular grid (the radius is equal to the grid spacing). This type of topologies is a good match for real-world deployments where the goal usually is a more or less regular coverage of the sensing area. We assume that two nodes can communicate with each other, if they are within a distance of at most $R_c = 100\text{m}$ (communication radius). Therefore, the communication graph is a *unit disk graph*.

Every sensor node possesses several different sensor types. Every type of sensor is uniformly distributed over the sensing area so that a certain percentage of nodes possess this sensor. Typically, the communication radius is larger than the sensing radius R_s [FK06b], therefore, we chose $R_s = \frac{1}{2}R_c$ as the sensing radius for all sensor types.

In the following subsections we show our simulation results for all algorithms described in the previous section. First, we evaluate the spatial grouping algorithms and then evaluate detection of complex events or processing of complex queries using the presented scheduling algorithm with different sets of concurrency constraints.

4.5.1 Space-bounded Quality of Sensing

In this subsection we evaluate spatial node grouping under two different settings. The first group of figures presented in Fig. 4.5 considers that every sensor node possesses exactly one sensor and there are four types of sensors distributed in the network. Thus, 25% of nodes in the network possess the same type of sensor. This setting is motivated by the bridge monitoring scenario discussed above, where it is quite energy-consuming and impractical to equip one sensor node with more than one complex sensor.

In Fig. 4.5a) we present the number of groups that possess all required sensor types built by the *FirstChoice* and *BestChoice* grouping algorithms combined with different selection rules and dispersion metrics. As can be seen from the graph, the number of complete groups increases with higher node densities and a greater number of deployed sensor nodes. Here, the *FirstChoice* algorithm dominates by constructing a slightly higher number of groups. In Fig. 4.5b), we analysed the cost of all algorithm combinations in terms of the number of sent packets per node in the network. The *BestChoice* algorithm is more expensive than the *FirstChoice* algorithm in all the respective combinations. The main reason for this is the iterative nature of the algorithm plotted in Fig. 4.5c) as the number of steps to reach convergence per node in the network. Additionally, it is worth mentioning, that both algorithms combined with the *Group* selection rule require more packets for distributed decision making among the group members than in combination with the *Leader* selection rule. Fig. 4.6a,b) present the average radius and its standard deviation of constructed groups relative to the communication range of the sensor nodes R_c. The *BestChoice* algorithm in all combinations generates the best solution. An interesting observation is that there is almost no difference in choosing *Group* selection rule over the *Leader* rule. Finally, we evaluate the coverage of the monitored area by the constructed groups and plot in Fig. 4.6c) the percentage of events that remain uncaptured by at least one constructed group. For this test, we generated 1000 events at random points of the monitoring area. We consider that an event is captured if there is at least one spatial group nearby such that the event is in a sensing range of all sensors of this group. Obviously, the complement to the percentage of uncaptured events represents the percentage of the covered area by the constructed groups. The percentage of uncaptured

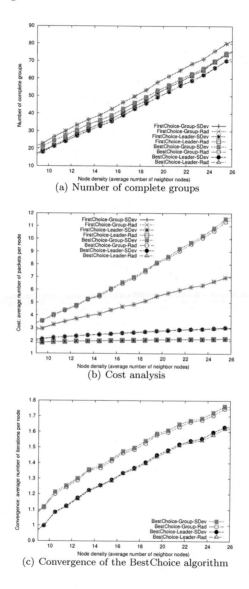

(a) Number of complete groups

(b) Cost analysis

(c) Convergence of the BestChoice algorithm

Figure 4.5: Evaluation of spatial grouping algorithms: First setting, evaluation set 1

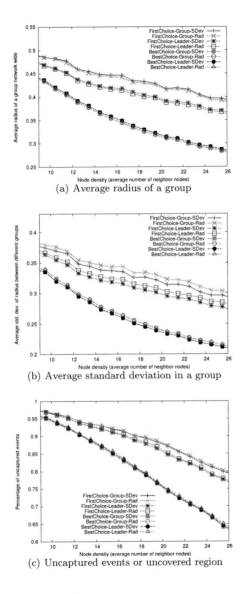

(a) Average radius of a group

(b) Average standard deviation in a group

(c) Uncaptured events or uncovered region

Figure 4.6: Evaluation of spatial grouping algorithms: First setting, evaluation set 2

events is very high in sparse networks with at most one sensor per sensor node. Again, the *BestChoice* algorithm outperforms the *FirstChoice* algorithm, as it tends to construct tighter groups and, therefore, increases the common area covered by all sensors of the group.

Fig. 4.7-Fig. 4.8 show the performance of spatial node grouping algorithms under the setting, that every sensor node can be equipped with more than one sensor. In this scenario, 50% of sensor nodes possess the same sensor type. This results in a higher number of complete groups plotted in Fig. 4.7a) than in the previous scenario. Moreover, due to the fact, that more nodes in the neighborhood possess the same kind of sensor, both grouping algorithms combined with the *Group* selection rule require higher number of sent packets per node. Therefore, the algorithms produce higher communication cost than under the previous setting. Interestingly, the algorithms combined with a *Leader* metric produce almost constant message overhead irrespective to the node density in the network, which makes this selection more applicable to dense scenarios than *Group*. Moreover, although the *BestChoice* algorithm requires several steps to converge, in combination with *Single* it does not produce a large increase in communication cost. Average radius and its standard deviation presented in Fig. 4.8a,b) give much better values than under the previous setting and the *BestChoice* grouping algorithm still considerably outperforms the *FirstChoice* algorithm. Small group radius and high number of successfully constructed spatial groups which include all required sensors to recognize an event lead to only 10% of uncaptured events and, therefore, to 90% of area coverage presented in Fig. 4.8c).

We refer to the percentage of uncaptured events as to *false negatives*. It is also interesting to evaluate the percentage of false positive event recognitions. If several events simultaneously happen outside of the sensing area of a particular group, but influence the values of individual sensor readings as if an event happens in the sensing area of a group, we say that our spatial grouping recognized a *false positive* event. However, our simulation results show that the percentage of false positives depends heavily on the number of simultaneous events and even under unfavorable settings is negligibly low (in a range of 0.5% for 100 simultaneous events).

4.5.2 Time-bounded Quality of Sensing

In this section we evaluate the presented scheduling algorithm. There are five types of sensors involved in the evaluation. The first three types of sensors are distributed uniformly among sensor nodes in the network so that 50% of sensor nodes possess the same type of sensor. The last two types of sensors

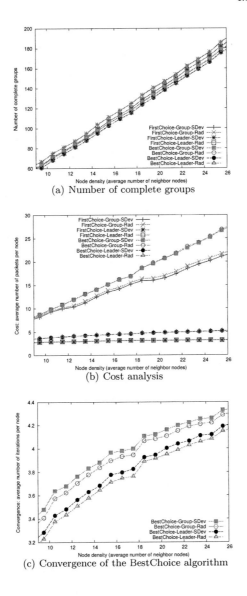

(a) Number of complete groups

(b) Cost analysis

(c) Convergence of the BestChoice algorithm

Figure 4.7: Evaluation of the spatial grouping algorithms: Second setting, evaluation set 1

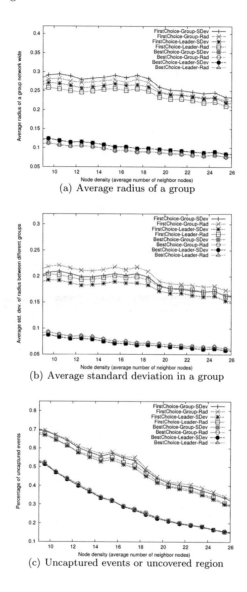

(a) Average radius of a group

(b) Average standard deviation in a group

(c) Uncaptured events or uncovered region

Figure 4.8: Evaluation of the spatial grouping algorithms: Second setting, evaluation set 2

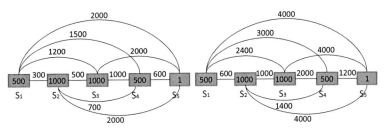

(a) "Hard" concurrency constraints   (b) "Medium" concurrency constraints

Figure 4.9: Two sets of concurrency constraints used in the evaluation of the scheduling algorithm: "hard" and "medium"

are distributed randomly over the network so that 60% of nodes have the same sensor. These sensors might be more common ones like temperature or humidity. The first four sensors have a sensing range of $R_s = \frac{1}{2}R_c$ and the last sensor $R_s = R_c$.

BestChoice and *FirstChoice* grouping algorithms combined with the *Group* selection rule and a *SDev* dispersion metric were used to build spatial groups. Moreover, we constructed two sets of concurrency constraints to evaluate the performance of scheduling algorithms: "hard" and "medium" presented in Fig. 4.9. We consider that the sensing tasks are ordered from left to right in the presented graphs. Notice, that none of these sets of concurrency constraints can be fulfilled when considering sequential scheduling on one sensor node equipped with all required sensors. Therefore, in both cases the schedule must consider the relocation of the sensing tasks to other sensor nodes in the spatial group.

In Fig. 4.10-Fig. 4.11 we present the evaluation results of the constructed schedules in every complete group in the network. Fig. 4.10a) plots the percentage of groups able to fulfil the schedule compared to the overall number of complete groups constructed by the spatial grouping algorithms. This graph shows a big difference in the difficulty of both schedules: up to 90% of groups were able to compute a valid "medium" schedule, whereas less than 30% of groups succeeded to execute the "hard" one. However, for both schedules the *BestChoice* algorithm performs worse than *FirstChoice*. Moreover, in Fig. 4.10b,c) we evaluate changes to the average spatial radius of the groups able to compute a valid schedule compared to the average spatial radius of all constructed groups. Only the worst groups constructed

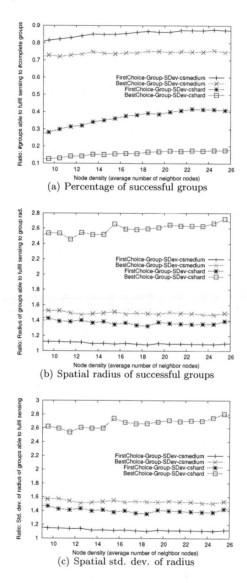

(a) Percentage of successful groups

(b) Spatial radius of successful groups

(c) Spatial std. dev. of radius

Figure 4.10: Spatial and temporal evaluation of the scheduling algorithm, evaluation set 1

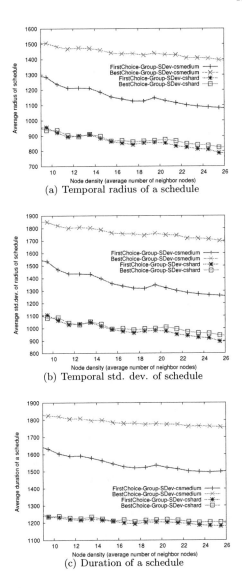

(a) Temporal radius of a schedule

(b) Temporal std. dev. of schedule

(c) Duration of a schedule

Figure 4.11: Spatial and temporal evaluation of the scheduling algorithm, evaluation set 2

by the *BestChoice* algorithms computed a valid schedule. The problem is, that the *BestChoice* algorithm constructs tighter groups than *FirstChoice* and, therefore, tends to group fewer nodes where more sensor types on each node are used. This shows that the *BestChoice* algorithm is better suited for events that require distributed space coordination whereas the *FirstChoice* algorithm is better suited for "hard" concurrency constraints and, therefore, for distributed time coordination.

In Fig. 4.11a-c) we evaluate the temporal characteristics of the constructed schedules: its average radius, standard deviation of the average radius in every group and average duration of a schedule. We define *radius of a schedule* as the maximum difference between the start execution times of the earliest and the latest task in the schedule. If the number of sensors in the group is equal to the number of sensor nodes in this group, the radius of a valid schedule equals 0. The *FirstChoice* algorithm outperforms the *BestChoice* algorithm also in the temporal characteristics of constructed schedules due to the reasons explained above.

4.6 Structure Analysis

In this thesis, we put a special emphasis on the spatial aspects of structures. Therefore, this section presents a discussion of structures built by the greedy and backtracking spatial grouping algorithms of the *ST-Grouping*.

Both algorithms converge, although the backtracking spatial grouping approach generates a convergence overhead. However, we show in evaluation section that this overhead is quite low. This makes greedy grouping more attractive for scenarios which involve limited node mobility. Both approaches are equally reconfigurable and stable when nodes join or leave the network. However, both algorithms do not track changes in link qualities unlike the routing algorithms. The algorithms are based on the existence of a link between two nodes or its absence. Due to the fact that the optimization criteria of spatial grouping is the construction of groups that are as tight as possible, bad quality links to the nodes located far away from each other become automatically unattractive for the algorithms. Therefore, the constructed group structures mainly contain good quality links between nodes within the same group.

Grouping algorithms generally construct local groups with low construction and maintenance overhead. Both variants of *ST-Grouping* algorithms require limited neighborhood knowledge for the construction and reconfiguration of a group. Naturally, the backtracking version of the algorithm generates additional message overhead, whereas the greedy spatial group construction algorithm constructs a local structure and is very scalable due to its independence of state information. The backtracking algorithm is more suitable for static scenarios: in the worst case, the backtracking procedure might affect all nodes in the network. Therefore, the structure generated by the backtracking spatial grouping is global but the generated groups have the smallest radius.

Flat grouping algorithms can often be found in mobile scenarios. For example, the greedy variant of *ST-Grouping* can handle limited node mobility. The spontaneous groups constructed in the *Sense-R-Us* system involve even less construction overhead and, therefore, support scenarios with a large number of mobile nodes.

The approaches described in this chapter are top-down: nodes join the group starting from the high priority member of the group to a low priority one.

4.7 Summary

In this chapter we have formulated the problem of time-bounded and space-bounded grouping in wireless sensor networks and provided a solution that allows complex event detection or query execution. Two cases were considered that require the distribution of sensing tasks among several nodes in vincinity: when a node is not equipped with all required sensors and when the event duration and the concurrency dependencies between sensing tasks preclude sequential sensing on one node. We have analyzed several spatial grouping algorithms for constructing groups of sensor nodes that can act together as one logical node equipped with all needed sensors to recognize an event. Additionally, we have provided a scheduling algorithm to enable the efficient relocation of sensing tasks to group members. Our evaluation results have shown that *ST-Grouping* provides good results for complex event detection even if no single sensor node is able to accomplish this task on its own.

4.8 Appendix: Terminology

$G(V, E)$	Undirected graph that models a sensor network
V	Set of nodes
E	Set of communication links between nodes
node 0	Base station or a sink node
$p : V \to \mathbb{R}^2$	Embedding function
$(x_i, y_i) \in \mathbb{R}^2$	Coordinates of node i on the plane
$A \subset \mathbb{R}^2$	Target area
$v : V \to 2^{\mathbb{S}}$	Types of sensors each node possesses
$\mathbb{S}$	Domain of sensor types used in the scenario
$Q = (S, R, D, C, \mathit{Pred})$	Query or event description
$S \subseteq \mathbb{S}$	Sensor types used in the query
$R : S \to \mathbb{R}$	Vector of sensing ranges for each sensor type
$D : S \to \mathbb{D}$	Vector of sensing times for each sensor type
$r \in \mathbb{R}$	Radius of a sensing area
$C : S \times S \to R$	Matrix of concurrency constraints
Pred	Predicate, evaluates combination of sensor values
$P \in \mathbb{R}^2$	Location of an event
$T_0 \in \mathbb{R}$	Start time of an event
$G_i \subseteq S \times V$	Group of sensors
k	Number of sensor types in a group
dist	Euclidean distance
$D(s_j)$	Duration of a sampling s_j
J_i^{local}	Local schedule
J_i	Group schedule
$\mathrm{Dur}(J)$	Duration of a schedule J
$\varphi(J)$	Temporal metric, expresses the badness of a schedule J
$\psi : S \times V \to \mathbb{R}$	Spatial dispersion metric

5 Boundary Recognition

Boundary recognition is an important and challenging issue in wireless sensor networks when no coordinates or distances are available. The distinction between inner and boundary nodes of the network can provide valuable knowledge to a broad spectrum of algorithms. The work described in this chapter tackles the challenge of providing a scalable and range-free solution for boundary recognition that does not require a high node density. We explain the challenges of accurately defining the boundary of a wireless sensor network with and without node positions and provide a new definition of network boundary in the discrete domain. Our solution for boundary recognition approximates the boundary of the sensor network by determining the majority of inner nodes using geometric constructions that guarantee that, for a given d, a node lies inside of the construction for a d-quasi unit disk graph model of the wireless sensor network. Moreover, such geometric constructions make it possible to compute a guaranteed distance from a node to the boundary. We present a fully distributed algorithm for boundary recognition based on these concepts and perform a detailed complexity analysis. We provide a thorough evaluation of our approach and show that it is applicable to dense as well as sparse deployments.

5.1 Preliminaries

Many WSN applications demonstrate the need for the extraction of such topological information [RPSS03, FKP$^+$04, FK06b]. Network lifetime is perhaps the most important issue in WSN. As the failure of boundary nodes results in reduced coverage, the load of these nodes should be reduced. For example, routing algorithms can exhaust the energy of the nodes that lie on the boundary of a hole [KFPF06]. The resulting coverage reduction might lead to a partitioning of WSN communication graph or missed events in the monitored region. However, it is possible to develop algorithms that adapt to the actual deployment using the distinction between boundary nodes and inner nodes. The knowledge about holes can also be used after an initial deployment or node failures to target specific areas with additional nodes.

In a large number of scenarios, for example in the environmental monitoring of vineyards, forests, or large warehouses, sensor readings differ heavily between the boundary and the center of the network. Sensor readings from the boundary nodes might influence the aggregation results considerably because they also capture events occurring outside of the monitored region of interest. Therefore, single sensor readings should be interpreted differently and aggregation should not be performed across inner and boundary nodes. A finer differentiation among nodes based on their distance to the boundary makes it possible to detect such an influence.

Whether a node is an inner or a boundary node might be crucial in object tracking scenarios. For example, when tracking events entering and leaving a region, boundary nodes might be involved in more complex sensing tasks whereas inner nodes might spend more energy on performing routing tasks. This lets boundary nodes play a special role that cannot be assigned prior to deployment. In addition, grouping nodes by nesting levels allows the definition of further security perimeters with different alert degrees.

Accurately defining the boundary of a wireless network is a challenge that should not be underestimated. [FK06b] provide an implicit definition of a network boundary in terms of nodes being close to the boundary of the continuous domain. [KFPF06, WGM06] define the boundary with the help of cycles. In this work we discuss the problem of defining the boundary in the discrete domain and its relation to two intuitive properties: uniqueness and continuity. We illustrate that this is a hard problem even with known node positions and show that the definitions found in prior work are incomplete. We then generalize the definition of boundary for the case where no location information is available and discuss its properties.

Our approach to the problem of boundary recognition presented in this chapter provides a close approximation of the generalized boundary without producing false negatives. Additionally, this boundary recognition approach is the first that is able to considerably relax the assumptions on node density and provides a good solution for both sparse and dense networks. Moreover, our result is a *generalization* of the approach described in [KFPF06]. Our approach is based on the recognition of inner nodes of the network and considers all other nodes to be part of the outer boundary or the boundary of a hole. We introduce geometric constructions, called patterns, that guarantee that a particular node lies inside of the pattern for all deployments of the sensor network with a given connectivity graph. Our patterns are generic, simple, parameterized and no global knowledge of the network connectivity graph is required to recognize them. These properties make our approach scalable and applicable to sparse networks. Moreover, many of the patterns allow additionally assigning to a node a guaranteed minimum distance to the boundary. Nodes with the same guaranteed distance from the boundary form a nesting level.

Although our patterns do not cover all nodes that lie inside of the network in all cases, simulation results show that the patterns are powerful enough to detect almost all inner nodes of the network and, therefore, provide a good approximation of the network boundaries. We provide pattern rules that considerably simplify the recognition of patterns and allow the algorithm to run in polynomial time.

5.2 Related Work

There is a strong need to extract spatial information of deployed sensor and ad-hoc networks without node coordinates. Even if distance information between the nodes is available, the problem of accurate node localization is NP-hard [AGY04]. However, a number of approaches provide reasonable approximations of different topological characteristics of the network such as the outer boundary of the network and boundaries of holes [FK06b, Fun05, WGM06, KFPF06], isolines or contours [FK06b] and medial axis lines [WGM06, BGJ05] or streets [KFPF06] that express topological levels based on the number of hops to the boundary.

Related work from the area of boundary recognition in sensor networks without location information can be classified into three groups based on the respective assumptions on node distribution, node density and the underlying communication model.

The approaches in the first group rely on a certain node distribution of the sensor nodes in the non-hole regions. For example, the approach described in [FKP+04] requires a uniform distribution of sensor nodes.

In the second group, a number of approaches [FK06b, Fun05, WGM06] present solutions for boundary recognition based on the assumption that the length of the shortest path between two nodes provides a reasonable approximation of the geometric distance between the nodes. However, this assumption requires a rather high average node degree in the network (in the range of 25) for the approaches to perform reasonably well [FK06b, Fun05]. The required node degree can be reduced to 10 if the topology conforms to a more regular node distribution like a grid or a perturbed grid [FK06b]. Under the unit disk graph assumption, sufficient node density and further assumptions on hole size and hole placement the algorithm marks the nodes close to the boundary with certain guarantees [FK06b]. In their previous work [Fun05], the authors additionally discuss that the success rate of their method decreases with the decrease of the parameter d when the network topology follows the d-quasi unit disk graph model. Another approach in this group [WGM06] also assumes that the distance among nodes can be approximated reasonably well based on the shortest path length and requires the lowest density of all approaches of this group with a node degree of 10 to 16. Such node densities are realistic for dense deployments [BLRS03].

The last group of approaches does not constrain the node distribution or make assumptions regarding node density but only sets constraints on the radio model of the sensor nodes. The unit disk graph model is a weak approximation of the properties of the wireless radio. Therefore, the more general d-quasi unit disk graph model is preferable [SW06]. The approach presented in [KFPF06] is the only work so far that provides a solution for the problem of boundary recognition based on the single assumption that the input network follows a d-quasi unit disk graph for a given $d \geq \frac{\sqrt{2}}{2}$. The algorithm searches for several types of patterns, so called "flowers", which are further extended and merged in the augmenting phase of the algorithm to form a boundary of the network. However, the presented flowers are extremely complex and in random topologies they only exist with a high probability if the average node degree is very high (20–30) [KFPF06,FK06a]. Moreover, a sensor node requires knowledge of its 8-hop neighborhood to be able to start searching for a flower. Evaluation results showed that this algorithm did not find a flower for network topologies with an average node degree smaller or equal to 10 [WGM06].

The approach presented in this work belongs to the last group and introduces the concept of patterns that are generic, simple and parameterizable by limiting the amount of neighborhood knowledge used. Therefore, even sparse networks with an average node degree of 4 include many simple patterns. The simplicity and generality of patterns considerably reduce the requirements on the node density of the network and the message complexity of pattern recognition. Flowers [KFPF06] form a tiny subset of our patterns. An additional feature of our pattern-based inner node recognition is that the majority of inner nodes are able to calculate a *guaranteed geometric distance* to the boundary of the network. We define a *nesting level* as a group of nodes with the same guaranteed geometric distance to the boundary which is the main difference to hop-based isolines or contours. Moreover, the cluster of nodes with the highest nesting level is located in the *geometric center* of the region, which is a stronger topological characteristic than the hop-based medial axis lines or streets.

5.3 The Boundary of a Sensor Network

The boundary of a sensor network is a complex spatial property even when a straight-line embedding of this graph into the two dimensional space is known (Terminology is summarized in Section 5.9). The problem of defining the boundary lies in the intuitive properties it should possess: uniqueness and continuity. Previous definitions of the term boundary of a network found in the literature fail to preserve these properties [KFPF06, WGM06, FK06b]. This section discusses the problem of defining the boundary in sensor networks both for the case when position information is available and for the case when it is not.

Let us first consider the case when a straight-line embedding $p : V \rightarrow \mathbb{R}^2$ of the network is given. This results in an arrangement of line segments where the endpoints correspond to the vertices and the segments correspont to the communication links. We say that p is a *d-quasi unit disk embedding* (*d*-QUDE) of G for a parameter $d \leq 1$ if both

$$uv \in E \Longrightarrow \| p(u) - p(v) \|_2 \leq 1$$
$$\| p(u) - p(v) \|_2 \leq d \Longrightarrow uv \in E$$

hold. G itself is called a *d-quasi unit disk graph* (d-QUDG) if such an embedding exists. A 1-QUDG is called a *unit disk graph* (UDG) and the corresponding embedding is a *unit disk embedding* (UDE). A *valid embedding* of the network is a *d*-QUDE for some fixed value of *d*.

According to the Jordan curve theorem, a simple closed curve divides the plane into two components – the outside and the inside. We call the outside the *infinite face* F_{inf}^p and the inside a *finite face* F^p. A sensor network can have several boundaries in an embedding: the outer boundary (border to the infinite face F_{inf}^p) and boundaries of holes (borders to finite faces $F^p \in F_{fin}^p$). These faces represent faces of interest defining uncovered regions in the network deployment. The elements of F_{fin}^p can be defined based on different spatial characteristics of a hole, e.g., the minimum size of its area, the length of its perimeter or the area of its convex hull [KFPF06].

The *perimeter* P_{F^p} of a face of interest F^p is defined as the set of segments of straight-line embeddings of communication links (edges) that belong to the face F^p. The perimeter P_{F^p} is both unique and continuous for a given embedding. Note that P_{F^p} does not have to include any end-point of an edge (node) as illustrated by the example in Fig. 5.1a). However, this purely edge-based perimeter is hardly useful in sensor networks. Instead, there is a need to define a *geometric boundary* B_{F^p} that approximates P_{F^p} based on nodes.

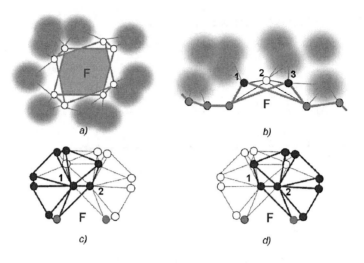

Figure 5.1: Problems related to the uniqueness and continuity properties of boundary definitions

We define the *geometric boundary* B_{F^p} as the set of nodes that belong to the perimeter P_{F^p} (if such nodes exist). Obviously, the geometric boundary defined this way is unique but *not continuous* in the sense that B_{F^p} does not necessarily form a connected cycle (see Fig. 5.1b)). For this reason, a number of other approaches define the boundary as the cycle that follows the perimeter of F^p [KFPF06, WGM06]. However, this definition does not possess the uniqueness property of the boundary. As an illustrating example, both the nodes 1 and 3 in Fig. 5.1b) might belong to the cycle. Moreover, such a boundary can even include nodes that are guaranteed to be inner nodes of the network for any valid embedding. We show an example in Fig. 5.1c) and d) for which it can be shown that nodes 1 and 2 lie inside of the network for any UDE. We highlight the subgraph that guarantees for node 1 to lie inside in c), and the subgraph that guarantees for node 2 to lie inside in d). We will later provide the proof of this fact (see Section 5.4). The continuity of the boundary is broken between the grey boundary nodes shown in the example if neither node 1 nor node 2 is used.

[FK06b] state that the goal of their algorithm is to mark a node near every point of the boundary of the continuous domain and that all nodes that are marked are near this boundary. This implicit definition of the network

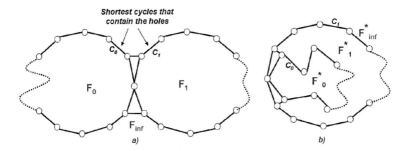

Figure 5.2: Problems related to hole definition

boundary in the discrete domain does neither preserve the uniqueness nor the continuity property, although the boundary defined in the continuous domain is both unique and continuous.

Recognizing a boundary *without position information* given a network connectivity graph requires the consideration of all valid straight-line embeddings of this graph. This leads to the following problems: First, the problem of finding valid embeddings of a graph is NP-hard even when a UDG is used to model the network [KMW04]. Second, the notion of holes in the deployment needs revision. Consider a straight-line embedding p of the network with a hole F^p of a certain size $size(F^p) \geq min_C$ (e.g., defined by the perimeter or the area). In this sense, it is impossible to construct a bijection between holes in different embeddings. Therefore, a hole is an *embedding-specific* geometric property.

In [WGM06], the authors approximate a hole F^p by the shortest cycle which contains the perimeter of the hole P_{F^p}. However, this approximation is unstable as well when looking at different valid embeddings. Consider a unit disk embedding p_1 of the network as shown in Fig. 5.2a). The embedded shortest cycles $p_1(C_0)$ and $p_1(C_1)$ contain the holes $F_0^{p_1}$ and $F_1^{p_1}$ respectively. Let the length of these cycles be $|C_0|$ and $|C_1|$ and assume that $|C_1| < |C_0|$. If we are interested in recognizing holes with a size (defined by the length of the shortest cycle) of at least min_C with $|C_1| < min_C < |C_0|$, then faces $F_0^{p_1}$ and $F_{inf}^{p_1}$ must be detected by the boundary recognition algorithm. In Fig. 5.2b) we show a different unit disk embedding p_2 of the same network. Here, two faces are contained in $p_2(C_1)$, which is the shortest cycle containing them. Consequently, in p_2 both faces are too small to qualify as holes as their shortest cycles are shorter than min_C. Note that it is possible that a shorter cycle contains a longer one even in a UDE (see Table. 5.1). For the

129

same reason, it is impossible to distinguish different hole boundaries without additional location information (e.g., the assumption that the shortest path approximates distance).

We now introduce our alternative definition of boundary that addresses the problems described above. If there exists a valid embedding p and a face F^p such that the shortest cycle in this embedding which contains P_{F^p} has a minimum length min_C, then F^p is an element of the *generalized set of holes* F_{fin}. We define the set of infinite faces F_{inf} that includes all infinite faces F_{inf}^p for all valid embeddings p. We define the *generalized boundary* of the network as the set of nodes such that for every node in this set there is a valid embedding p in which this node belongs to the geometric boundary of a face $F^p \in F_{fin} \cup F_{inf}$. The generalized boundary is unique (unless the connectivity graph changes). Moreover, it is minimal as it only contains nodes that belong to the outer perimeter or the perimeter of a hole in at least one valid embedding. However, the generalized boundary is not continuous as can be seen in Fig. 5.1c) and d) in which the highlighted nodes 1 and 2 never belong to the generalized boundary as explained later in this chapter.

Any reasonable boundary acquired without location information includes the nodes of the generalized boundary. In this work, we use the property of the generalized boundary that its complement consists of all nodes that do not belong to the outer boundary or the boundary of a hole for any valid embedding. Our approach approximates the generalized boundary of the network by recognizing nodes that always lie inside of the network for any valid embedding and assumes that all other nodes belong to the generalized boundary.

5.4 Patterns

As motivated above, our approach recognizes inner nodes – nodes that do not belong to a boundary for any valid embedding. We introduce the concept of *patterns* – subgraphs that guarantee for any valid d-QUDG embedding that a certain node lies inside of the pattern. This inner node is the *seed* of the pattern. Let us now consider the UDEs of the subgraphs as depicted in Fig. 5.3a) and c). At first sight, both subgraphs seem to fulfill these requirements but as shown by the counter-examples in Fig. 5.3b) and d), it is not guaranteed that the seed S lies inside of the construction for *all* valid UDEs. We show some real patterns in Fig. 5.3e-h). Fig. 5.3h) is the smallest pattern for UDGs we were able to find: Node S only needs the knowledge of the communication links between its direct neighbors to detect

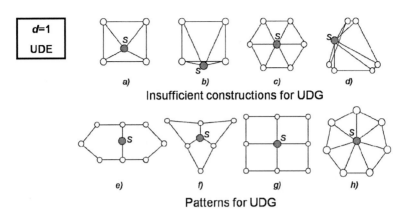

Figure 5.3: a-d) Insufficient constructions for UDG; e-h) Patterns for UDG

this pattern. Below we provide a few supporting lemmas and a separate proof of the pattern property for the constructions presented in Fig. 5.3f) and h). Later in this section we show that the examples Fig. 5.3e) and g) are also patterns.

Lemma 5.4.1. *Consider a subgraph $H \subset G$ consisting of four vertices $v, w, x, y \in V$ where $xy, yv, vw, wx \in E$ and no other edge exists between these vertices. A UDE of this subgraph results in a quadrangle on the plane. If a vertex z is embedded inside of this quadrangle, it must be adjacent to at least two adjacent vertices of this subgraph.*

Proof. Let o be the intersection of the two diagonals yw and xv (see Fig. 5.4a)). Consider the vertex x. It is connected to the vertices y, w. If we consider a unit circle centered at x, it will include both vertices y, w and, therefore, the complete line segment yw. Thus, every vertex located inside of the triangle Δ_{xyw} must be connected with node x in any valid UDE. Thus, a vertex inside of any triangle $\Delta_{xoy}, \Delta_{yov}, \Delta_{vow}, \Delta_{wox}$ must be adjacent to at least two corresponding adjacent vertices in H. □

Lemma 5.4.2. *The graph in Fig. 5.3f) is a pattern in UDE.*

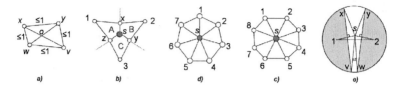

Figure 5.4: Illustrations to Lemmas 5.4.1, 5.4.2 and 5.4.5

Proof. Consider Fig. 5.4b). If rays are constructed from vertex S along the edges to x, y, z, the space is subdivided into three open faces: A, B and C. A unit circle centred at z intersects the segments Sx and Sy, which implies that if 1 belongs to the open face B, then it must lie inside of the quadrangle $xSy2$. In this case, additional edges $1S$ or 12 must exist based on Lemma 5.4.1. Analogously, 1 cannot belong to the open face C.

Corresponding arguments hold for node 2 and node 3. Therefore, nodes 1, 2 and 3 always lie in the faces A, B and C respectively. Thus, node S lies inside the construction. □

Lemma 5.4.3. *Consider a triangle Δ_{xyz} with $\| xy \|_2 \leq 1$ and $\| yz \|_2 \leq 1$ and $\angle xyz \leq \frac{\pi}{3}$. Then $\| xz \|_2 \leq 1$.*

Proof. Continue yx and yz so that $\| yx' \|_2 = 1$ and $\| yz' \|_2 = 1$. Assume $\| xy \|_2 \leq \| yz \|_2$. Based on the Jensen's inequality for convex functions, $\| xz \|_2 \leq \| xy \|_2 \leq 1$ or $\| xz \|_2 \leq \| xz' \|_2$. In the second case, $\| xz' \|_2 \leq \| yz' \|_2 = 1$ or $\| xz' \|_2 \leq \| x'y' \|_2 \leq 1$. □

Lemma 5.4.4. *Consider a subgraph $H \subset G$ consisting of three vertices $x, y, z \in V$ where $xy, yz, zx \in E$. A UDE of this subgraph results in a triangle on the plane. If a vertex v is embedded inside this triangle, it must be adjacent to all three vertices x, y, z.*

Proof. Unit circles centered at x, y, z respectively include all points in the triangle. □

Lemma 5.4.5. *The graph in Fig. 5.3h) is a pattern in UDE.*

Proof. Assume vertex S lies outside of the cycle constructed from vertices $1, 2, 3, 4, 5, 6, 7$ (cf. Fig. 5.4d)). All vertices must lie within a unit circle centered at S. Consider the edge 12 and the two middle verticals to the line segments $1S$ and $2S$ which partition the circle into 3 parts (cf. Fig. 5.4e)). The vertices $4, 5, 6$ have no edges to vertex 1 or vertex 2. Every point inside of the grey parts is closer to the nodes 1 or 2 than to the node S. Therefore, the vertices $4, 5, 6$ must lie inside the white part. If some of the vertices $4, 5, 6$ lie above the edge $1, 2$ and some lie below, at least one edge between $4, 5, 6$ intersects the edge $1, 2$. Since there are no edges between vertices $4, 5, 6$ and vertex 1 or vertex 2, this is not possible based on Corollary 5.4.9. None of the vertices $4, 5, 6$ can lie in the quadrangles $1xSv$ or $2wSy$, since every point in these quadrangles is less than 1 away from nodes 1 and 2 respectively. None of them can lie inside the triangle $\Delta 1S2$ since every point in the triangle is adjacent to 1 and 2 based on Lemma 5.4.4. Since there is no edge between vertices 4 and 6, they cannot both lie in ΔvSw based on Lemma 5.4.3 ($\angle \alpha \leq 60$). If all vertices $4, 5, 6$ lie inside ΔxSy, then S lies inside the construction.

$\square$

Corollary 5.4.6. *Consider a graph consisting of $n + 1$ vertices $V = S \cup \{x_0 | 0 \leq i < n\}$ with edges $E = \{x_i x_{(i+1) \bmod n} | 0 \leq i < n\} \cup \{Sx_i | 0 \leq i < n\}$. The graph is a pattern in UDE if $7 \leq n \leq 11$.*

Proof. This follows directly from Lemma 5.4.5. The maximum value for $n = 11$ results from the fact that it is not possible to construct a chordless cycle of more than 11 vertices where the UDE of all 11 vertices is in a unit circle. $\square$

Note that the pattern in Fig. 5.4c) that was used to show the non-continuity of the boundary for UDGs is also covered by Corollary 5.4.6.

So far we have shown a few distinct pattern examples. However, every pattern has a very specific structure and, therefore, only a few nodes in a random network might be seeds of such patterns. We are interested in the generalization of this approach and the possibility to describe a powerful family of patterns. Additionally, our goal is to formulate the pattern recognition rules for recognizing the individual patterns that belong to this family. In this section we provide our generic pattern rules for the UDG model of a network and later extend these rules for the more general d-QUDG model, which better captures the properties of wireless links [SW06]. We prove that all constructions generated by these rules, including the constructions shown in Fig. 5.3e,g), are indeed patterns and, therefore, guarantee for the seed to lie inside for *any* valid embedding. Our approach works for all d-QUDGs with $d \geq \frac{\sqrt{2}}{2}$. This lower bound for d is fundamental for the mathematical concepts of our approach and results from Lemma 5.4.7. This lemma has been proven for UDE in [BK98] and improved for d-QUDE with $d \geq \frac{\sqrt{2}}{2}$ by [KFPF06]. We give here the proof presented in [KFPF06].

Lemma 5.4.7. *Let x, y, w, v be four different nodes in V, where $xy \in E$ and $wv \in E$. Assume the straight-line d-QUDE (for $d \geq \frac{\sqrt{2}}{2}$) of xy and wv intersect. Then at least one of the edges in $F = \{xv, vy, yw, wx\}$ is also in E.*

Proof. Assume $p(x) \neq p(y)$; otherwise the proof of the lemma is trivial. Let $a = \|p(x) - p(y)\|_2 \leq 1$. Consider two circles of common radius d with their centers at $p(x)$, resp. $p(y)$. The distance between the two intersection points of these circles is $h = 2\sqrt{d^2 - \frac{1}{4}a^2}$. If F and E were disjoint, $p(w)$ and $p(v)$ had both to be outside the two circles, however for $d \geq \frac{\sqrt{2}}{2}$ it follows that $h \geq 1$. Because of the intersecting edge embeddings, $\|p(w) - p(v)\|_2 > h \geq 1$, which would contradict $wv \in E$. $\qquad \square$

In order to provide the precise description of pattern rules for UDGs and d-QUDGs, we start with the terminology which also summarizes several important previous results.

5.4.1 Terminology

$D(V_D, E_D)$ is defined to be a *vertex-induced subgraph* of $G(V, E)$, if $V_D \subseteq V$, $E_D \subseteq E$ and the following condition holds: $\nexists v_i, v_j \in V_D | v_i v_j \in E$ and $v_i v_j \notin E_D$. This means that for a chosen subset of nodes all edges between them are preserved and no others are added.

$N_k(D)$, the k-hop neighborhood of the vertex-induced subgraph $D \subseteq G$, is the vertex-induced subgraph of G that includes all nodes reachable from at least one node in D within a maximum of k hops. We set $N_0(D) = D$.

We model a sensor network using a d-QUDG as defined in Section 5.3 to capture radio irregularities to some extent. The smaller the value of d, the more general and realistic is the model.

Let C be a vertex-induced subgraph of G and $V_C = \{v_0, v_1, \ldots, v_{k-1}\} \subset V$ be a sequence of $k > 3$ distinct vertices such that $v_i v_{(i+1) \bmod k} \in E_C, \forall i = 0 \ldots k-1$ and no other edge exists between any two of these vertices. We refer to C as a *chordless cycle* of length $|V_C| = k$. A d-QUDE of a chordless cycle C is a polygon which decomposes a plane into the infinite face and at least one finite face. Every point in the infinite face is defined to lie *outside* of this polygon. There exist multiple finite faces if the embedded chordless cycle is self-intersecting.

We use the following properties to check whether a connected subgraph can be placed inside of a chordless cycle for a d-QUDE. Consider a chordless cycle $C \subset G$ and a connected vertex-induced subgraph $D \subset G \setminus N_1(C)$. A *maximum independent set* $I_C(D) = \{v_i\} \subset V_D$ with respect to C is a maximum subset of V_D such that: $\forall v_i, v_j \in I_C(D), v_i v_j \notin E$. The elements of an independent set are called *independent nodes*. Since the distance between any pair of independent nodes is at least d (in any d-QUDE), an independent set requires a certain *minimum* area on the plane to place the subgraph D. The embedding of a chordless cycle in the plane results in a polygon with a limited *maximum* area that depends on the length of the chordless cycle. As defined in [KFPF06], the number $fit_d(k)$ is the maximum number of independent nodes that can be placed inside of a chordless cycle C of length $|V_C| = k$ for a d-QUDE. The *independent set property* (ISP) for a d-QUDE with $d \geq \frac{\sqrt{2}}{2}$ holds for a chordless cycle C and a connected vertex-induced subgraph D if

$$|I_C(D)| > fit_d(|V_C|).$$

This means that there is not enough space in the chordless cycle to place all independent nodes of D inside of it. Additionally, Lemma 5.4.7 guarantees that the embedding of D must lie *completely* outside of the embedding of C if the ISP holds.

5.4.2 Patterns in UDG

We now propose our generic pattern rules for the UDG model. We present a formal definition and then explain the individual conditions including the terms *extended independent set property* and *critical intersection*.

We first introduce a *weak pattern* $P(S, 1)$ for UDG ($d = 1$) and later present a *strong pattern* $P^*(S, d)$ for the d-QUDG model. We define a weak pattern $P(S, 1) = C_0 \cup \cdots \cup C_{n-1}, 2 \leq n \leq 5$ with respect to a seed node S as a vertex-induced subgraph of G composed of chordless cycles C_i such that $\forall i, j = 0 \,..\, n - 1$, $i \neq j$ the following conditions hold:

1. $S \in V_{C_i}$

2. $|V_{C_i \cap C_j \cap N_1(S)}| = \begin{cases} 1, & j \neq (i \pm 1) \bmod n \\ 2, & j = (i \pm 1) \bmod n \wedge n > 2 \\ 3, & j = (i \pm 1) \bmod n \wedge n = 2 \end{cases}$

3. For $C_i, (P(S, 1) \setminus N_1(C_i))$ the *extended independent set property* holds

4. For $C_i, \bigcup_{j \neq i} C_j$ there exists no *critical intersection*

The main idea behind the weak patterns is to have a cycle and ensure that the seed has enough connections to the nodes of the cycle to keep it inside (pattern conditions (1) and (2)). The pattern conditions (3) and (4) guarantee, that although the cycle and the connections might intersect, the seed node still lies inside of the construction. In the pattern condition (3), the extended independent set property checks if the ISP holds for a cycle C_i and the extended neighborhood of $P(S, 1) \setminus N_1(C_i)$. This guarantees that C_i cannot include all other cycles that compose the pattern simultaneously. Condition (4) checks that the cycles do not lie partially in each other. After introducing the necessary terminology, we provide formal definitions and examples of the extended independent set property and the critical intersection test.

To be able to reason about patterns, we have to define a few more terms, which are also illustrated in the example pattern in Fig. 5.6. We call $V_{P(S,1)} \cap V_{N_1(S)}$ the set of *anchors*. The number of anchors is equal to the number of cycles the pattern comprises, which we call the *pattern cardinality*. If a pattern consists of at least three cycles, then each pair $C_i, C_{(i+1) \bmod n}$ shares one anchor. We call this anchor the *common anchor* CA_i. If a pattern is composed of exactly two chordless cycles, both anchors are shared by both cycles and we deterministically define (e.g., by node ID) CA_0 and CA_1. Now consider the vertex-induced subgraph $T_A = N_1(C_i) \cap N_1(C_{(i+1) \bmod n}) \cap (C_i \cup C_{(i+1) \bmod n}) \setminus S$. This subgraph is generally not connected. We define the *conjunction* J_i between two cycles $C_i, C_{(i+1) \bmod n}$ to be the connected component in T_A that includes CA_i. The nodes that compose the conjunction are called *conjunction nodes*. Finally, we define the *outer cycle* of a pattern as the connected vertex-induced subgraph with the set of edges $E_{P(S,1)} \setminus E_{\bigcup J_i}$.

To motivate the need for pattern conditions (3) and (4), we show different possible embeddings of the bold chordless cycle C_i in Fig. 5.5 for a combi-

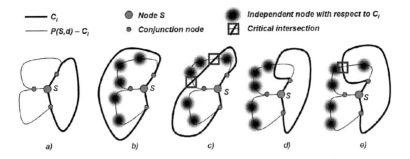

Figure 5.5: Combinations of three chordless cycles

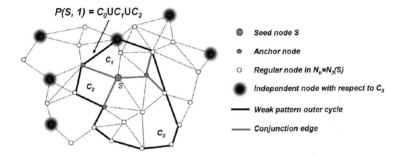

Figure 5.6: Extended independent set property

nation of three cycles. There are three possible relations of one cycle to the others: it may contain them (b), it may intersect them (c,d,e) and it may lie on a different side of S (a,d,e). In cases b) and c) C_i is called *reflected*. If S lies outside of the construction, then either one cycle contains all others or there is a *critical intersection* of at least two chordless cycles. A critical intersection occurs when an independent set of a vertex-induced subgraph is partitioned by the intersection with a chordless cycle. In Fig. 5.5 the example b) is rejected (is not sufficient to be a pattern) because one cycle contains all others and examples c) and e) are rejected because of a critical intersection. The intersection in example d) is not critical and, therefore, both a) and d) are valid patterns.

We use the *extended independent set property* (eISP) to check if a cycle C_i can contain all other chordless cycles in a d-QUDE with $d \geq \frac{\sqrt{2}}{2}$. Vertex-

137

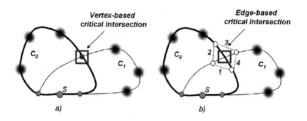

Figure 5.7: Types of critical intersections

induced subgraph $\bar{C}_i = N_h(S) \setminus N_1(C_i)$ generally consists of multiple connected components. The parameter h specifies the considered neighborhood knowledge. Compute the size of a maximum independent set for each connected component that contains at least one node of $P(S,d) \setminus N_1(C_i)$. If the sum of these sizes is greater than $fit_d(|V_{C_i}|)$, then C_i cannot contain all other chordless cycles. Note that using the standard ISP would only allow us to calculate a maximum independent set for $P(S,d) \setminus N_1(C_i)$ (without considering the whole neighborhood $N_h(S)$, the so-called *extension*). The eISP is especially important for complex patterns with long cycles since the number of independent nodes that can fit in a chordless cycle grows faster than the cycle length (see Table 5.1).

We illustrate how the eISP works in Fig. 5.6 for a weak pattern $P(S,1) = C_0 \cup C_1 \cup C_2$. The ISP does not hold for C_0, $P(S,1) \setminus N_1(C_0)$ because $P(S,1) \setminus N_1(C_0)$ contains only one independent node with respect to C_0 and there is enough space in a cycle of length $|V_{C_0}| = 9$ (see $fit_1(9)$ in Table. 5.1) to place this node inside for some UDE without any changes to the connectivity graph. However, the eISP holds since a connected component in $\bar{C}_0 = N_h(S) \setminus C_0$ (for this example, $N_h(S) = G$) that includes this independent node contains a maximum independent set of size $6 > fit_1(9) = 2$.

If S lies outside of the construction but the eISP holds, then the embeddings of at least two cycles must intersect. Since the eISP holds, both cycles must contain at least one independent node with respect to each other. We show examples of such constructions consisting of two cycles in Fig. 5.7. We distinguish between *vertex-based* (a) and *edge-based* (b) intersections. In order to detect a *critical intersection*, we require that either the cycles share at least one node Fig. 5.7a) or that at least one of the dotted edges (1–4) in Fig. 5.7b) exists. Lemma 5.4.7 shows that at least one edge exists for a d-QUDE with $d \geq \frac{\sqrt{2}}{2}$. We show that at least two edges exist for a UDE with the following Lemma 5.4.8.

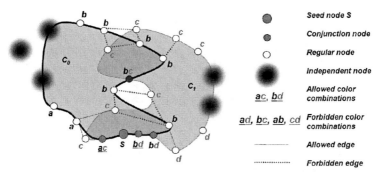

Figure 5.8: Coloring test

Lemma 5.4.8. *Let x, y, w, v be four different nodes in V, where $xy \in E$, $wv \in E$ and $xw \in E$. Assume the straight-line UDE of xy and wv intersect. Then at least one of the edges in $F = \{xv, yw\}$ is also in E.*

Proof. Assume $p(x) \neq p(y) \neq p(w) \neq p(v)$; otherwise the proof of the lemma is trivial. Let $a = \parallel p(x) - p(y) \parallel_2$. Consider two circles of common radius d with their centers at $p(x)$ and $p(y)$ respectively. The distance between the xy segment and the intersection points of these circles is $\frac{h}{2} = \sqrt{d^2 - \frac{1}{4}a^2}$. As F and E are disjoint, $p(w)$ must lie outside of the circle with the center at $p(y)$ and $p(v)$ has to lie outside of the circle with the center at $p(x)$. Because of the intersecting edge embedding, for $d \geq 1$, $\parallel p(w) - p(v) \parallel_2 > \sqrt{(\frac{h}{2})^2 + (d - \frac{a}{2})^2} = \sqrt{2d^2 - ad} \geq 1$, which contradicts that $wv \in E$. $\square$

Corollary 5.4.9. *Let x, y, w, v be four different nodes in V, where $xy \in E$ and $wv \in E$. Assume the straight-line UDE of xy and wv intersect. Then at least one of the following is true: $xw, wy \in E$ or $wy, yv \in E$ or $yv, vx \in E$ or $vx, xw \in E$.*

Proof. This follows directly from Lemma 5.4.7 and Lemma 5.4.8. $\square$

Consider a pattern $P(S, d) = \bigcup_{i=0}^{n} C_i$. The intersection of a chordless cycle C_i and $\bigcup_{j \neq i} C_j$ is *critical* if at least one of the following is true:

- $\exists C_j \in \bigcup_{j \neq i} C_j$ such that $C_j \setminus N_1(C_i)$ consists of at least two connected components;

- $\exists$ a conjunction J_i between C_i and $C_j \in \bigcup_{j \neq i} C_j$ $(CA_i \subset J_i)$ such that $\exists$ a common anchor $CA_k, k \neq i | CA_k \subset J_i$.

For the second kind of critical intersection, in case a pattern is composed of two cycles, both common anchors belong to the same conjunction, as it is the case in Fig. 5.8.

We detect critical intersections by coloring the chordless cycles. We have to execute the following procedure for every chordless cycle C_i and $\bigcup_{j \neq i} C_j$. We color C_i starting at its two anchors with two different colors. Additionally, we switch to a new color each time we encounter an independent node with respect to $\bigcup_{j \neq i} C_j$. We color the other cycles of $P(S, d)$ the same way starting at their anchor nodes and change the color after each independent node with respect to C_i. S is then the only uncolored node. The vertices of the conjunctions between $C_i, C_{(i+1) \bmod n}$ define the *allowed* color combinations. Every node and every edge connecting nodes of C_i and $\bigcup_{j \neq i} C_j$ is inspected. If the color combination is not allowed, then we speak of a *critical intersection*.

In Fig. 5.8, we color the nodes of two overlapping chordless cycles with colors a, b, c and d. The conjunctions define the color combinations ac and bd to be allowed. In figure we show a few examples of allowed and forbidden edges. All forbidden edges indicate that the critical intersection may occur.

Lemma 5.4.10. *If node $S \in V_G$ is the seed of a weak pattern $P(S, 1) \subseteq G$, then S is an inner node for any UDE of G.*

Proof. Assume a UDE such that S lies outside of $P(S, 1)$. Then either at least one chordless cycle of $P(S, 1)$ is reflected or at least one conjunction intersects the outer cycle. Assume C_i is a reflected cycle in $P(S, 1)$. Let us color $C_i, \bigcup_{j \neq i} C_j$. According to the eISP C_i cannot contain all other chordless cycles in $P(S, 1)$. Therefore, C_i intersects $C_j \subset P(S, 1)(j \neq i)$. However, as no coloring conflicts are found, the intersection between C_i and C_j must have a color combination allowed by the two conjunctions of C_i. Therefore, no independent node is located between node S and the nodes that belong to the intersection. So, all independent nodes of $P(S, 1) \setminus C_i$ lie inside of C_i, which violates the third pattern condition.

From Lemma 5.4.8 it follows that a conjunction J_i can only intersect one edge of the outer cycle which lies in $N_1(J_i)$ and connects $C_i \setminus J_i, C_{(i+1) \bmod n} \setminus J_i$. No two conjunctions can intersect the same edge and from the fourth pattern condition follows that no two conjunctions can intersect each other. If the

seed lies outside of the pattern and no cycle is reflected, then there is one
cycle that contains all others. □

5.4.3 Patterns for d-QUDG

After the definition of patterns for UDG in the previous subsection, we now
present our extended approach that supports d-QUDG for $d \geq \frac{\sqrt{2}}{2}$. The
simple patterns for UDG presented in Fig. 5.3 are not sufficient for the d-
QUDG model with $d < 1$. We show counter examples in Fig. 5.9b) and
d) for the UDG-only patterns shown in Fig. 5.9a) and c). We also show
patterns for d-QUDG with $d \geq \frac{\sqrt{2}}{2}$ in Fig. 5.9e-g). The examples f) and
g) are taken from [KFPF06] and illustrate an interesting difference to our
approach. In [KFPF06] these very complex patterns are used to detect a
group of guaranteed inner nodes (highlighted in the figure), whereas our
approach is able to detect each of these inner nodes individually. By using
simpler as well as more complex patterns our approach is more general and
more powerful. All of these patterns are covered by the following extended
pattern definition.

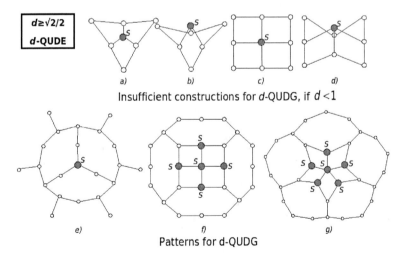

Figure 5.9: a-d) Insufficient constructions for d-QUDG, $d < 1$; e-g) Patterns
for d-QUDG (f,g) from [Kröller et al. 2006])

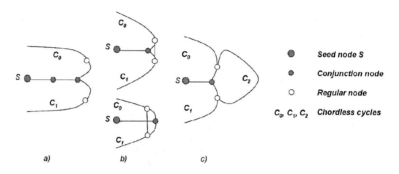

Figure 5.10: Fifth condition of a strong pattern

We define a *strong pattern* $P^*(S,d) = C_0 \cup \cdots \cup C_{n-1}$, $2 \leq n \leq 8$ with respect to a seed node S as a vertex-induced subgraph of G composed of chordless cycles C_i such that $\forall i,j = 0 \ldots n - 1$:

1-4) $P^*(S,d)$ fulfills the conditions of the weak pattern definition for the given value of d

5) One of the following conditions holds for each conjunction J_i between the pair of chordless cycles $C_i, C_{(i+1)\bmod n}$:

    a) $|V_{J_i \setminus S}| \geq 2$

    b) $|V_{J_i \setminus S}| = 1$ and an edge exists between
        $N_1(J_i \setminus S) \cap C_i$ and $N_1(J_i \setminus S) \cap C_{(i+1)\bmod n}$

    c) $|V_{J_i \setminus S}| = 1$ and a weak pattern exists for $V_{J_i \setminus S}$ that includes
        $C_i, C_{(i+1)\bmod n}$

Fig. 5.10 illustrates the three cases of the fifth pattern condition of a strong pattern. The reason why a weak pattern $P(S,d)$ does not suffice in a d-QUDE for $d < 1$ is that Lemma 5.4.7 does not preclude the possibility that a chordless cycle is self-intersecting (e.g. Fig. 5.9b) and d)). This is only guaranteed for UDE by Lemma 5.4.8. Therefore, a strong pattern must ensure that the seed S still lies inside of the strong pattern for any embedding even if a chordless cycle is self-intersecting.

Lemma 5.4.11. *If node $S \in V_G$ is the seed of a strong pattern $P^*(S,d) \subseteq G$, then S is an inner node for any d-QUDE of G with $d \geq \frac{\sqrt{2}}{2}$.*

Proof. The proof for strong patterns exactly follows our proof for weak patterns. There is only one additional point to show: Although conjunctions may intersect the outer cycle of a strong pattern $P^*(S, d)$, the seed S is still guaranteed to lie inside of it. Assume S lies outside of the construction. Let $C_i \subset P^*(S, d)$ be a chordless cycle. It follows from the fifth condition of a strong pattern that $|V_{C_i}| > 4$. The conjunction J_i between $C_i, C_{(i+1) \bmod n}$ can intersect edges of the outer cycle of the strong pattern in $C_i \cap N_2(J_i)$ and in $C_{(i+1) \bmod n} \cap N_2(J_i)$. However, these vertex-induced subgraphs do not overlap for any pair of conjunctions, which follows from the fifth condition of a strong pattern and Lemma 5.4.7. Since no independent node with respect to C_i is in $N_1(J_i)$, this intersection is not critical. Therefore, there is a chordless cycle that contains all others. This violates the third pattern condition and contradicts the assumption. □

5.4.4 Pattern Properties

There are several important properties of weak and strong patterns that can be used to derive further spatial information of a sensor network and to optimize the pattern recognition algorithm.

Distance guarantees: Both weak and strong patterns guarantee that the seed lies inside of the pattern. However, a strong pattern additionally ensures that the seed has no direct connection (edge) to the outer cycle of the pattern. Therefore, the seed is at least $dist = \sqrt{d^2 - \frac{1}{4}}$ away from every edge of this outer cycle. Thus, strong patterns can additionally provide *distance guarantees* for their seeds.

Nesting levels: We show in Section 5.5.2 how to accumulate guaranteed distances in order to designate nesting levels for sensor nodes.

Inclusion property: For the set of patterns the following *inclusion property* holds

$$\text{if } P(S, d) \text{ then } P(S, q), \forall q \geq d.$$

as long as there exists a valid q-QUDE for $P(S, q)$. This property is important for applying the pattern concept in real-world deployments where the exact value of d is not known.

Maximum pattern cardinality: The size of a maximum independent set of $N_1(S)$ for a node S is limited by $\left\lfloor \frac{\pi}{\arcsin \frac{d}{2}} \right\rfloor$ (5 for a UDG, 8 for the d-QUDG model with $d = \frac{\sqrt{2}}{2}$). These numbers correspond to the maximum number of vertices in a regular polygon – with an edge length greater than

d – that can be placed in a unit circle. This limits the maximum number of chordless cycles in a pattern and restricts the search depth.

Discreteness: In a UDE both weak and strong patterns can be used. Weak patterns only guarantee that the seed lies inside of the construction whereas strong patterns additionally provide a guaranteed minimum distance of $\frac{\sqrt{3}}{2}$ from the outer cycle of the pattern. However, if we consider a d-QUDE with $d \in [\frac{\sqrt{2}}{2}, 1)$, only strong patterns work. This *discrete* behavior of patterns results from Lemma 5.4.7 and Lemma 5.4.8: According to Lemma 5.4.7, there are only two possible relations between two edges $xy, vw \in E$ for a d-QUDG with $d \in [\frac{\sqrt{2}}{2}, 1)$. If $xv, xw, yv, yw \notin E$, then x and y are at least $\sqrt{d^2 - \frac{1}{4}}$ away from vw. If *at least* one of the edges xv, xw, yv, yw exists, then there might be an embedding where xy, vw intersect. There is one more possibility in UDE: if *exactly* one of the edges xv, xw, yv, yw exists, xy, vw cannot intersect according to Lemma 5.4.8, but x or y can be arbitrarily close to vw.

Soundness: Our approach is *sound* as the patterns covered guarantee that the corresponding seed nodes lie inside of the network for any d-QUDE with $d \geq \frac{\sqrt{2}}{2}$.

Incompleteness: While being able to describe a family of simple as well as arbitrarily complex patterns, this concept does not cover the whole set of patterns (e.g., the pattern shown in Fig. 5.3h)). Therefore, our approach is *incomplete*. However, we show in the evaluation section that our pattern rules are powerful and general enough to recognize a large number of guaranteed inner nodes for dense as well as for sparse topologies.

5.5 Boundary Recognition Algorithm

Having laid out the mathematical foundations and necessary conditions for patterns, we now present our algorithm for boundary recognition and its complexity analysis.

The goal of the *boundary recognition algorithm* is to find weak and strong patterns in the network. It also assigns a level to every node that indicates its distance to the boundary. If a node is guaranteed to lie inside of the network, level 1 is assigned (UDG only). If the node is additionally guaranteed to be at least $dist = \sqrt{d^2 - \frac{1}{4}}$ away from the boundary, then level 2 is assigned. All other nodes are assumed to belong to the generalized boundary and receive level 0.

Our algorithm is parameterized with d, which specifies the d-QUDG model. The range of d is limited to $\frac{\sqrt{2}}{2} \leq d \leq 1$, which is a hard bound for our algorithm resulting from Lemma 5.4.7. The second parameter is h, which specifies the h-hop neighborhood used for finding patterns. We limit the maximum length of chordless cycles to $2h + 1$. This implies that the minimum chordless cycle length that defines the generalized set of holes is $min_C = 2h + 2$. In order to reduce the time, space and message overhead for dense networks, h should be chosen based on the average node degree in the respective network. We provide guidelines for selecting reasonable values of h in the evaluation section.

After the boundary recognition algorithm has finished, it is executed again using only those nodes that have been identified as seeds of strong patterns. We assign the nesting level 3 (UDE only) or 4 to nodes that are the seeds of weak or strong patterns in this round. We repeatedly execute the algorithm, each time reducing the examined graph and incrementing the levels, as long as strong patterns are found.

5.5.1 Boundary Recognition

The boundary recognition algorithm executes the following steps for each node S in order to find a weak (UDE only) or strong pattern by checking the pattern conditions.

1) Gather the connectivity graph of the h-hop neighborhood N_h.

2) Find all chordless cycles of maximum length $2h + 1$ in N_h that include S (condition 1).

3) Construct valid combinations of chordless cycles (condition 2) and perform:

    a) The extended independent set test (condition 3).

    b) The critical intersection test (condition 4).

    c) The strong pattern test (condition 5).

We now explain each step in detail and analyze their respective time, space and message complexities.

1) Gather the h-hop connectivity graph

Every node broadcasts a message containing its ID with a time to live (TTL) of h. When a node receives such a message from another node, it appends its ID (constructing a path), decrements the TTL and forwards the message. The message complexity of this step for one node is $O(h^2 n_{max})$ where n_{max} is the maximum node degree in N_h. Constructing the connectivity graph of N_h runs in $O(h^4 n_{max}^3)$ time and requires $O(h^2 n_{max}^2)$ space.

2) Find chordless cycles

In this step, we perform a depth first search starting at S to find all chordless cycles in the connectivity graph $N_h(S)$. The maximum search depth is limited by the maximum length of a cycle $2h+1$. This step runs in $O(n_{max}^{2h+1})$ time. We have to store the chordless cycles in memory for later being able to construct the chordless cycle combinations needed to find patterns. However, it is difficult to establish a tight upper bound on the number of chordless cycles. This number clearly depends on h and the maximum node degree in the neighborhood. We have to estimate an upper bound for the number of chordless cycles in an h-hop neighborhood by the number of paths of length smaller than $2h+1$ that start at S. This number is clearly greater than the number of chordless cycles. Therefore, the definitely over-estimated space complexity is $O(n_{max}^{2h+1})$.

The space complexity of finding chordless cycles dominates the space complexity of the whole algorithm. Additionally, the number of chordless cycles determines how many combinations of cycles are possible and how often the rather expensive tests for the remaining pattern conditions have to be performed. Therefore, the number of chordless cycles is the determining factor of the time and space complexity of the complete algorithm. To reduce the number of cycles used in later tests, we define a *similarity metric* for chordless cycles and avoid storing multiple similar ones. If one cycle cannot be used to construct a pattern, it is unlikely that a very similar cycle can be used successfully. To take advantage of that, we developed μ-*filtering* for two chordless cycles C_i and C_j that both contain S. For a chordless cycle C, we define the *center* node $c_S(C)$ relative to $S \in C$ as the node in C that has the greatest hop distance to S. If the length of the cycle is odd, this node is unambiguous. If the length is even, we choose the center node deterministically (e.g., by node ID). Two cycles are considered similar, if they share the same anchors and the center node of one cycle is also part of the other:

1) $C_i \cap N_1(S) = C_j \cap N_1(S)$ – share the same anchors

2) $c_S(C_i) \in V_{C_j} \vee c_S(C_j) \in V_{C_i}$ – the center node of one cycle is also part of the other

If two cycles are considered similar we only keep the longer cycle in order to increase the probability of constructing a strong pattern.

Each chordless cycle has two anchor nodes and exactly one center node. The μ-filtering method allows for only one chordless cycle with the same anchor nodes and the same center node. Therefore, the number of chordless cycles after μ-filtering can be estimated with $n_{cyc} = O(h^2 n_{max} C(n_{max}, 2)) = O(h^2 n_{max}^3)$ where $C(n, k)$ is the binomial coefficient. Consequently, the space complexity is $O(h^3 n_{max}^3)$. The search for chordless cycles including μ-filtering runs in $O(n_{max}^{2h+4} h^2)$. As we show in the evaluation section, this very simple but efficient similarity metric does not degrade the quality of the boundary recognition and reduces both the time and the space complexity of the complete algorithm significantly.

3) Construct valid combinations of chordless cycles

In this step, we check the second pattern condition by constructing the valid combinations of chordless cycles using depth first search (DFS). We perform the remaining pattern tests as described in the next paragraphs. DFS runs in $O(n_{cyc}^{\text{card}_{max}})$ time and requires $O(n_{cyc})$ space where card_{max} is the maximum pattern cardinality (5 for UDE, 8 for d-QUDE with $d = \frac{\sqrt{2}}{2}$). We show in the evaluation that by using reasonable parameter values it is possible to reduce the maximum number of chordless cycles to construct a pattern to 2 and 3 (instead of 5 and 8) for UDE and d-QUDE respectively without degrading the result.

3a) Extended independent set test

Since the problem of finding a maximum independent set is NP-hard, we use the following greedy algorithm to approximate such a set. Consider a connected vertex-induced subgraph $D = N_h \setminus C_i$ for which a maximum independent set is to be computed. We search for a node v with a minimum node degree and choose this node as an element of the independent set. This step is performed repeatedly for the vertex-induced subgraph $D = D \setminus N_1(v)$ until $D \setminus N_1(v) = \{\}$. Note that the independent set constructed this way is maximal but not necessarily maximum. The time complexity of this step is $O(|V_D|^2 \, log \, |V_D|) = O(h^2 n_{max}^2)$.

3b) Critical intersection test

As discussed above, we perform the critical intersection test by coloring the nodes of a potential pattern $P(S, d)$. The algorithm consists of the following steps for every chordless cycle C_i of $P(S, d)$:

1. Determine the set of *unrelated* nodes in C_i and in $P(S, d) \setminus C_i$ that have no edge to any node of the other set.

2. Color the nodes of C_i and $P(S, d) \setminus C_i$ as described in Section 5.4.2.

3. Determine the two color combinations allowed by the two conjunctions of C_i.

4. If vertex-based or edge-based illegal color combinations exist, then reject $P(S, d)$.

Determining the set of unrelated nodes in step 1 and coloring all nodes (step 2) both run in $O(h^2)$ time and require $O(h)$ additional space. The running time of checking for illegal color combinations (step 4) lies in $O(h^2)$ and no additional space is required.

3c) Strong pattern test

For checking whether the conjunctions fulfill the fifth strong pattern condition, we only consider the first two possibilities of the fifth condition. This is done in $O(1)$ without any additional space.

We now present the overall complexities of the boundary recognition algorithm for a single node using μ-filtering and with limiting the pattern cardinality to 3. These optimizations are also used in the evaluation. The resulting time complexity is $O(n_{max}^{2h+4} h^2)$, the space complexity is $O(n_{max}^3 h^3)$, and the message complexity is $O(n_{max} h^2)$, where h is the depth of the neighborhood N_h and n_{max} is the maximum node degree in N_h. These complexity values hold for $h \geq 4$.

5.5.2 Nesting Levels

After the boundary recognition algorithm is completed, we execute it again for all nodes of level 2. This corresponds to constructing a vertex-induced subgraph $G' \subset G$ composed of the nodes of level 2 and using G' as input to the pattern recognition algorithm. However, since each level 2 node still only has to gather the connectivity information of its h-hop neighborhood,

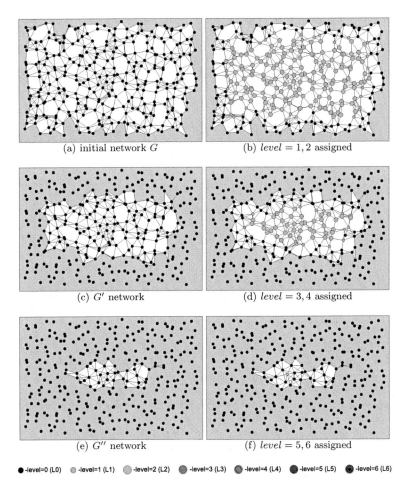

Figure 5.11: Example process of constructing nesting levels

no global knowledge is required. After the second run of the algorithm, the seeds of the weak patterns (UDE only) and of the strong patterns are assigned the levels 3 and 4 respectively. Consequently, nodes of level 4 are at least $2 \cdot dist$ away from the boundary. The boundary recognition algorithm is executed repeatedly as long as seeds of strong patterns (resulting in higher levels) are found. Since in each round the examined graph is smaller than in the previous round, the algorithm is guaranteed to terminate. We show the nesting level process for an example topology in Fig. 5.11. The resulting assignment of nesting levels is shown in Fig. 5.13b).

Since the algorithm does not produce any false positives when recognizing inner nodes, it is possible to repeat the boundary recognition algorithm and increase the guaranteed distances to the boundary. The pattern rules do not consider any nodes or edges to nodes outside of the pattern. If a node fails to find a strong pattern because our approach is incomplete, it might prevent other nodes from increasing their level in the next round. However, any pattern found by the algorithm is valid.

5.6 Evaluation

The primary goal of the evaluation is to show that our approach is general enough to support both sparse and dense deployments. We also investigate empirical values that determine time and space costs of the different steps of our algorithm and conclude with guidelines on how to select the most appropriate parameter values.

5.6.1 Setup

For our experiments, we concentrate on two types of topologies: random and grid-based. We use *random* topologies (uniform distribution) to show that our approach does not rely on any assumptions concerning the regularity of node positions, as required by some previous approaches. We use *grid-based* topologies to create more realistic scenarios: the nodes are placed randomly inside of circles arranged in a regular grid (the radius is equal to the grid spacing). This type of topology better matches real-world deployments where the goal usually is a more or less regular coverage of the sensing area. Therefore, even in the case of autonomous deployments of sensor nodes for example with the help of helicopters or other vehicles, instructions exist concerning movement trajectories and deployment points that assume some kind of grid overlay.

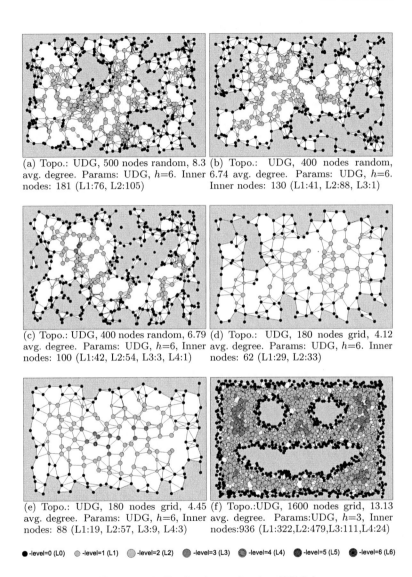

(a) Topo.: UDG, 500 nodes random, 8.3 avg. degree. Params: UDG, $h=6$. Inner nodes: 181 (L1:76, L2:105)

(b) Topo.: UDG, 400 nodes random, 6.74 avg. degree. Params: UDG, $h=6$. Inner nodes: 130 (L1:41, L2:88, L3:1)

(c) Topo.: UDG, 400 nodes random, 6.79 avg. degree. Params: UDG, $h=6$, Inner nodes: 100 (L1:42, L2:54, L3:3, L4:1)

(d) Topo.: UDG, 180 nodes grid, 4.12 avg. degree. Params: UDG, $h=6$. Inner nodes: 62 (L1:29, L2:33)

(e) Topo.: UDG, 180 nodes grid, 4.45 avg. degree. Params: UDG, $h=6$, Inner nodes: 88 (L1:19, L2:57, L3:9, L4:3)

(f) Topo.:UDG, 1600 nodes grid, 13.13 avg. degree. Params:UDG, $h=3$, Inner nodes:936 (L1:322,L2:479,L3:111,L4:24)

● -level=0 (L0)   ◉ -level=1 (L1)   ◯ -level=2 (L2)   ◉ -level=3 (L3)   ◉ -level=4 (L4)   ● -level=5 (L5)   ◉ -level=6 (L6)

Figure 5.12: Qualitative evaluation (UDGs)

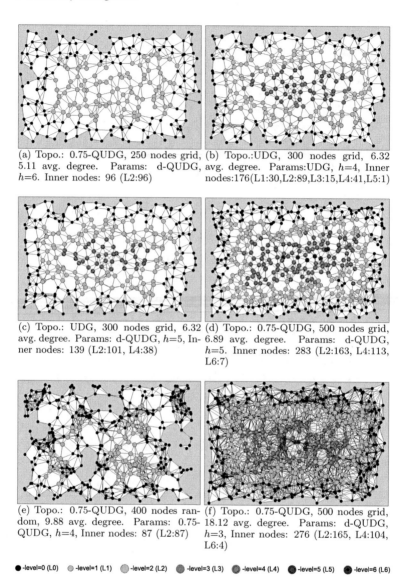

(a) Topo.: 0.75-QUDG, 250 nodes grid, 5.11 avg. degree. Params: d-QUDG, h=6. Inner nodes: 96 (L2:96)

(b) Topo.:UDG, 300 nodes grid, 6.32 avg. degree. Params:UDG, h=4, Inner nodes:176(L1:30,L2:89,L3:15,L4:41,L5:1)

(c) Topo.: UDG, 300 nodes grid, 6.32 avg. degree. Params: d-QUDG, h=5, Inner nodes: 139 (L2:101, L4:38)

(d) Topo.: 0.75-QUDG, 500 nodes grid, 6.89 avg. degree. Params: d-QUDG, h=5. Inner nodes: 283 (L2:163, L4:113, L6:7)

(e) Topo.: 0.75-QUDG, 400 nodes random, 9.88 avg. degree. Params: 0.75-QUDG, h=4, Inner nodes: 87 (L2:87)

(f) Topo.: 0.75-QUDG, 500 nodes grid, 18.12 avg. degree. Params: d-QUDG, h=3, Inner nodes: 276 (L2:165, L4:104, L6:4)

● -level=0 (L0) ◉ -level=1 (L1) ◯ -level=2 (L2) ◍ -level=3 (L3) ◍ -level=4 (L4) ● -level=5 (L5) ● -level=6 (L6)

Figure 5.13: Qualitative evaluation (d-QUDGs)

The probability that a link exists between two nodes is calculated by $\frac{1-s}{1-d}$ for a distance s between two nodes with $d \leq s \leq 1$. While our approach supports asymmetric links as long as the connectivity graph is a valid d-QUDG, we only experiment with symmetric links in our topologies.

We vary the network wide average node degree between 2 and 20 taking into account the results discussed in [BLRS03] where values between 3 and 9 are suggested as reasonable for networks composed of 50 to 500 nodes.

n	4	5	6	7	8	9	10	11	12	13
$fit_1(n)$	0	0	0	1	1	2	3	4	5	7
$fit_{\uparrow 1}(n)$	0	0	1	1	2	3	4	5	7	8
$fit_{\uparrow\sqrt{2}/2}(n)$	1	1	2	3	5	7	8	10	13	17

Table 5.1: Independent set property (ISP): values of fit_d for different d

We use the values shown in Table 5.1 for the fit_d-function. Since determining these values corresponds to solving the packing problem, we approximate the values assuming a hexagonal and square packing of nodes for UDE and d-QUDE respectively. Hexagonal and square packings provide packing densities of $\frac{\pi}{2\sqrt{3}}$ and $\frac{\pi}{3\sqrt{2}}$. It is known that a hexagonal packing is the most dense packing for the infinite face. However, even by applying both packings to estimate the maximum number of circles that can be located inside of a polygon, we cannot guarantee that the values in the table are not underestimated. Nevertheless, we have chosen the values deliberately high because we consider the whole N_h neighborhood for the extended independent set test. Using the eISP instead of the ISP increases the number of detected patterns considerably. Our experience shows that constructions are usually not rejected because of the eISP test. A critical intersection is more common than one cycle containing all the others.

5.6.2 Qualitative Evaluation

As explained before, our algorithm approximates the generalized boundary of a network by detecting the nodes that belong to its complement, i.e., the set of nodes that lie inside the network for every d-QUDE. Therefore, the nodes that belong to the geometric boundary of an embedding are included in the set of detected boundary nodes but cannot be distinguished from other nodes that are not part of the boundary in this particular embedding without location information. We are not aware of any way to reliably determine all nodes that belong to the generalized boundary. Therefore, the only reasonable way to evaluate the quality of our approach is to visually inspect the result. We examined a large number of results covering a wide range of parameters. Although at first sight some nodes appear to be inner nodes for any obvious embedding, closer examination reveals a possible embedding where they belong to the boundary.

In Fig. 5.12 and Fig. 5.13 we present several examples of network topologies (UDG and d-QUDG) processed by our algorithm with different node distributions and a wide range of different average node degrees that represent a wide spectrum of possible network deployments. Since the evaluation of previous approaches uses the UDG model, we first show several UDG deployments. Fig. 5.12a-c) are examples of sparse random deployments of UDGs (average node degree 6.74 - 8.3) which require the nodes to have information of their 6-hop neighborhood. More regular grid-based UDG deployments shown in Fig. 5.12d) and e) with an even lower average node degree of 4.12 also require the knowledge of the 6-hop neighborhood. In Fig. 5.12f) we show a dense topology with artificially created holes. The high average node degree allows achieving good results considering only the 3-hop neighborhood when looking for patterns.

We now continue the evaluation of our approach using the more realistic d-QUDG model with $d \geq \frac{\sqrt{2}}{2}$. Note that only even levels are meaningful as nesting levels for the d-QUDG model. We show a sparse grid-based 0.75-QUDG network deployment with an average node degree of 5.11 in Fig. 5.13a). A slightly higher value of the average node degree allows decreasing the amount of required neighborhood knowledge (Fig. 5.13c-f)). Since no holes exist in the deployment in the examples (Fig. 5.13d) and f), the nodes with the highest nesting level of 6 approximate the center of the network. Examples Fig. 5.13b) and c) show the results of the same topology processed assuming a UDE (b) and a d-QUDG model (c) to illustrate that there is only a small difference in the number of nodes of corresponding nesting levels despite the higher requirements on $fit_d(k)$. Fig. 5.13d) represents a much larger deployment area with the same average node degree as in Fig. 5.13c). Therefore, the "thickness" of the boundary and the distance guarantees are the same in both figures despite the different visual impression the figures give. Fig. 5.13e) shows the performance of our approach on a randomly generated 0.75-QUDG. We present a very dense topology in Fig. 5.13f) that allows us to use only the minimum possible neighborhood knowledge (3-hops) for searching strong patterns in d-QUDE. For UDE it is even possible to only search the 2-hop neighborhood if nesting levels are not required.

As explained above, [KFPF06] uses a small number of complex patterns that require knowledge of the 8-hop neighborhood and that rarely occur in networks with an average node degree between 20 and 30. They show an example in [FK06a] where only 138 disjoint flowers are found in a UDG network of 60 000 nodes. Additionally, [WGM06] showed example networks with an average node degree smaller than 10 where no patterns were found at all by the approach introduced in [KFPF06]. Even the approach with the lowest requirements on node density so far [WGM06] provides good results only for node densities of 10–16 for UDG. Our evaluation shows that our approach works well in sparse networks even with an average node degree of 4.

5.6.3 The Cost of Pattern Recognition

After evaluating the result quality of our boundary recognition algorithm in the previous subsection, we now present the empirical analysis of several values that determine the cost incurred by our algorithm. We show that the results of the complexity analysis in Section 5.5 considerably overestimate the actual cost of running the algorithm.

Fig. 5.14a) and b) show the average number of chordless cycles found depending on the average node degree for a large number of topologies. Since boundary nodes find fewer chordless cycles than inner nodes (see Fig. 5.15), the ratio between boundary nodes and inner nodes determined by the network size directly influences the number of cycles. For that reason, we chose three different network sizes with 100, 300 and 500 nodes and constructed 20 grid-based topologies for each size. We varied the transmission range in each topology in order to obtain different average network wide node degrees and computed the average number of chordless cycles for different values of $h \in \{2, 4, 6\}$. In Fig. 5.14a) we show the average number of chordless cycles found by a node (note the logarithmic scale). The average number of chordless cycles after μ-filtering is presented in Fig. 5.14b) (linear scale). We evaluated the efficiency of μ-filtering by computing the ratio between the number of cycles left after μ-filtering and the total number of cycles which is plotted in Fig. 5.14c). Our analysis shows that the efficiency of μ-filtering increases with the average node degree and with higher values of h. Therefore, μ-filtering decreases the space and time requirements of the complete pattern recognition algorithm significantly.

After finding the relevant set of chordless cycles, the next step of the pattern recognition algorithm is to search for a valid pattern by combining the chordless cycles. This search stops as soon as a strong pattern is found. This prevents inner nodes from unnecessarily searching through all possible

155

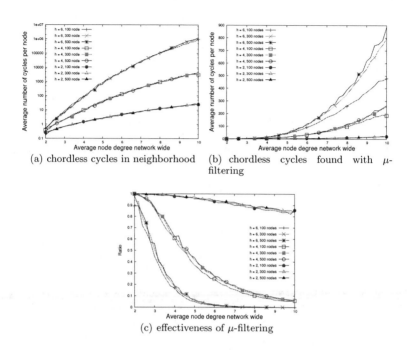

(a) chordless cycles in neighborhood

(b) chordless cycles found with μ-filtering

(c) effectiveness of μ-filtering

Figure 5.14: Evaluation of μ-filtering

combinations. The number of chordless cycle combinations that form a pattern in UDE and d-QUDE is limited by the maximum pattern cardinality. However, it is generally cheaper to check for a potential pattern consisting of fewer cycles. More importantly, the number of combinations grows exponentially with the maximum pattern cardinality considered. It is interesting to evaluate the benefit of a higher pattern cardinality. For the network shown in Fig. 5.13b-c) we calculated the number of nodes for which a pattern exists that is composed of $n_{combi} + 1$ chordless cycles, while no pattern exists that involves only n_{combi} chordless cycles. In Fig. 5.16 we show the percentage of nodes that recognized a pattern consisting of a certain minimum number of cycles for values of h between 2 and 6. This provides two important insights: On the one hand, there is a certain value of $h = h'$ for which almost all inner nodes find a pattern so that there is no benefit in further increasing h. On the other hand, for $h = h'$ there exists a pattern consisting of only 2 (UDE) or 3 (d-QUDE) cycles for nearly all inner nodes. The saturation

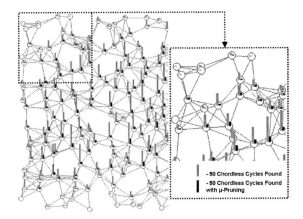

Figure 5.15: Number of chordless cycles found in different regions

of the number of detected inner nodes with increasing values of h motivates the need for guidelines for parameter selection depending on the density of the sensor network. Such guidelines are described later in this section.

5.6.4 Parameter Selection and Adaptation

It is important to select reasonable parameter values for h and the pattern cardinality tailored to the properties of the deployed network in order to achieve both a good result quality and a low overhead of the algorithm. On the one hand, selecting a small value for the minimum generalized hole size in very sparse networks makes nearly all nodes part of boundaries of holes or of the outer boundary. On the other hand, trying to recognize only very large holes in dense deployments forces the algorithm to process large subgraphs of the connectivity graph of the network.

For that reason it is necessary to select reasonable parameters in order to ensure algorithm performance while minimizing unnecessary complexity.

The main parameter of the system is h which defines the depth of the neighborhood that has to be considered as well as the minimum size of a hole $2h + 2$. Obviously, h should be chosen based on the density of the network. We have investigated the influence of the density on the average number of chordless cycles (per node) with a given length. We chose the grid-based

157

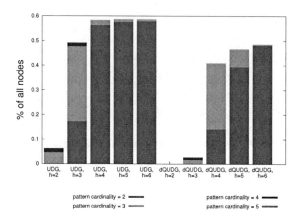

Figure 5.16: Required pattern cardinality

topology (to reduce the variance) shown in Fig. 5.13b) and varied the transmission range to obtain different average node degrees. In Fig. 5.17a) and b) the average number of cycles with a given length is plotted against the average node degree. Values without (logarithmic scale) and with μ-filtering (linear scale) are shown.

On the one hand, it is obvious that in a network with an average node degree of 4 almost no cycles of length ≤ 13 can be found. Therefore, it does not make sense to search for patterns in a neighborhood of fewer than 6-hops. On the other hand, sufficiently high node densities allow only examining the 2-hop or the 3-hop neighborhood and still find enough chordless cycles to construct a pattern. Note that the reasonable minimum size of a hole also correlates with the node density. Our experience shows that 30 chordless cycles (after μ-filtering) are usually enough for sparse networks with average node degrees smaller than 8 and that 100 cycles are enough for denser networks. A larger number of cycles is required for dense networks because the cycles start and end at a larger number of anchor nodes. Note that the minimum chordless cycle length is 4 for weak patterns and 5 for strong patterns (this results from the 5th condition of a strong pattern).

Since the variance of the average node degree is relatively small in grid-based topologies, it is possible to use the same value of h for the whole network. In random topologies one can find in the same network both areas with a very high average node degree and areas with a very low average node degree. We show an example of such a random network topology in Fig. 5.18. The

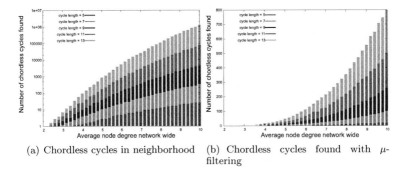

(a) Chordless cycles in neighborhood   (b) Chordless cycles found with μ-filtering

Figure 5.17: Parameter selection guidelines

same value of h was selected for the complete network. Our algorithm finds nearly all inner nodes in the left part where the value of h is sufficient for the average node degree of this area. However, the sparser area in the right part of the figure requires a greater value of h. This motivates the need for adapting the value of h to the local density of the region, which we plan to investigate as part of future work.

5.7 Structure Analysis

This section is dedicated to the analysis of the properties of boundary recognition algorithms. We compare the proposed method and the algorithms discussed in the related work section. A summary of this analysis is presented in Table 5.2.

The boundary recognition algorithms discussed in this chapter are generally stable. However, only algorithms that use local knowledge are easily reconfigurable. For the algorithms by *Funke* [FK06b] and *Wang* [WGM06], reconfiguration is problematic. For each reconfiguration, the algorithms have to be started from the beginning and proceed through all nodes in the sensor network. Moreover, these algorithms result in a good approximation of the network boundaries only for very dense network deployments. They produce unexpected and wrong results when applied to sparse networks.

All discussed boundary recognition algorithms are generally scalable although the requirements concerning the amount of network knowedge differs considerably. Their overhead results from either flooding the whole network

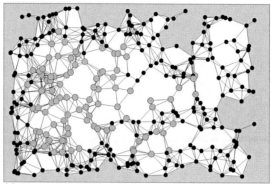

(a) Topo.: 0.75-UDG, 330 nodes rnd., 7.67 avg. degree.
Params: 0.75-UDG, h=5, Inner nodes: 87 (L2:87)

Figure 5.18: Example topology motivating the need for adaptation

starting from a fixed small number of nodes or from gathering the connectivity information of the kth neighborhood, which corresponds to a limited flooding starting from every node in the network.

Although the boundary without location information can be seen a local structure, not all algorithms are able to extract the structure only with local knowledge. Therefore, the class of algorithms that requires flooding of the whole network produces increased maintenance overhead and is unsuited for scenarios that include node mobility. The other solutions including the approach developed in this work have also limited support for mobility due to the relatively high computational complexity of these algorithms.

Our boundary recognition algorithm and the algorithm by *Kröller* proceed bottom-up by recognizing provably inner nodes of the network as described in Chapter 5. The algorithms by *Funke* and *Wang* are neither top-down nor bottom-up, rather they operate on shortest paths in the network which are assumed to be a good approximation of the distances between individual nodes. Such hybrid solutions are not easily reconfigurable and are less scalable.

Our boundary recognition approach is the only parameterized approach. The provided parameter defines the minimum size of a cordless cycle to be considered as a hole; it is naturally different for dense and sparse sensor networks and can, therefore, be specified tailored to a concrete deployment. It is also possible to adapt the value of this parameter based on the local

Property	Saukh	Kröller	Funke	Wang
Stab./Reconfig	+	+	-	-
Convergence	+	+	problem	problem
Param./Adapt	+	-	-	-
Temp./Static	S	S	S	S
Coordinates	-	-	-	-
Mobility	-	-	-	-
Scalability	+	+	+	+
Overhead	high	high	high	high
Top-down/Bottom-up	BU	BU	hybrid	hybrid

Table 5.2: Classification of boundary extraction algorithms and obtained structures

node density.

5.8 Summary

With this approach we have tackled the challenge of providing a graph-oriented definition of the boundary of a sensor network. We have defined the *geometric boundary* for the case when the embedding of the communication graph in the plane is known and the *generalized boundary* for the case when no embedding is given. We have shown that the generalized boundary is unique unless the communication graph changes, but in the general case is not continuous.

We have presented an algorithm that without location information computes a close approximation of the generalized boundary by recognizing inner nodes of the network and considering all other nodes to belong to the generalized boundary. Our approach is based on the d-quasi unit disk graph model for radio propagation and supports any $d \geq \frac{\sqrt{2}}{2}$. We are able to guarantee that all nodes recognized as inner nodes lie inside of the network for any d-quasi unit disk embedding for a given d. We also provide additional discrete distance guarantees to the boundary called nesting levels. The correctness of our solution for inner node recognition based on generic pattern rules is mathematically proven. We have presented our algorithms built upon these concepts and have shown in the evaluation that our optimizations significantly reduce time and space complexities without degrading the result. We have also shown that our approach works well on dense and sparse topologies and, therefore, can successfully be applied to a wide range of scenarios. The algorithm can be parameterized based on a given node density in order to further reduce the message, time, and space overhead while still providing good results. We provided guidelines for these parameter value selections.

Note that $\frac{\sqrt{2}}{2}$ is a hard limit for d and cannot be reduced by any incremental work on our solution. Although our generic pattern rules do not cover the complete set of patterns, the mathematical properties and the quality of the results especially for sparse networks illustrate the power and wide applicability of our approach.

5.9 Appendix: Terminology

$G(V, E)$	Undirected graph that models a sensor network
V	Set of nodes in a sensor network
E	Set of communication links between nodes in a sensor network
$uv \in E$	Communication link between nodes u and v
$p : V \to \mathbb{R}^2$	Straight-line embedding of the network into 2D
$0 \le d \le 1$	Parameter in the d-QUDG model
F_{inf}^p	Infinite face
F^p	Finite face
P_{F^p}	Perimeter of a face F^p
B_{F^p}	Geometric boundary of a face F^p
C	Chordless cycle
F_{fin}	Generalized set of holes
$F_{fin} \cup F_{inf}$	Generalized boundary
$P(S, d)$	Pattern
S	Seed of a pattern
$N_k(D)$	k-hop neighborhood of the vertex-induced subgraph $D \subseteq G$
$I_C(D)$	Maximum independent set
$fit_d(k)$	Maximum number of independent nodes that can be placed inside of a chordless cycle C
CA	Common anchor
J_i	Conjunction between two cycles $C_i, C_{(i+1) \bmod n}$
h	Algorithm parameter, maximum neighborhood knowledge
$2h + 2$	Minimum hole length
n_{max}	Maximum node degree in N_h

5 Boundary Recognition

6 Convex Groups

Mobile ad-hoc networks have been long proposed for rescue scenarios to support and coordinate the efforts of helpers. Low power wireless sensor networks are a natural extension of this approach. They can provide valuable environmental data enriched with location information to deepen the insight of the operational area. Gateways between these two communication paradigms are necessary to facilitate the collaboration of both systems. We study such multi-sink wireless sensor network scenarios and explore the use of *Convex Groups* to efficiently disseminate location dependent information for example for query distribution. *Convex Groups* show significant advantages in terms of message overhead compared to straightforward approaches without sacrificing connectivity. They do not exhibit high computational complexity and handle node mobility as well as gateway mobility gracefully. The evaluation results presented in this chapter show the broad applicability of convex grouping.

6.1 Introduction

Most newly developed applications for wireless sensor networks require the cooperation of a wireless sensor network (WSN) with a more powerful mobile ad-hoc network (MANET). Such applications rely on the use of contextual data extracted from the sensor network. Either each MANET device communicates directly with its surrounding sensor network, which requires an additional WSN-compatible communication adapter, or some devices act as gateways (sinks) and supply the others with context information over the ad-hoc network.

The combination of these two different types of systems - large scale, an extremely resource-constrained sensor network on the one hand and a powerful ad-hoc network on the other hand - creates new challenges that need to be addressed from the ground up. The most fundamental challenge deals with the development of efficient communication and cooperation paradigms between these network types.

In the AWARE project, several applications that involve the cooperation between MANETs and WSNs are studied. One example is the fire fighting scenario where, in case of fire, sensor nodes are deployed with unmanned aerial vehicles (UAVs) to provide context information. The collected environmental data is used to assist the operation of fire fighters and rescue units as well as the mission planning of the available UAVs.

This scenario requires a flexible architecture which enables easy access to context information and allows to incorporate the different types of MANET devices used in this setting. Preinstalled cameras, UAVs, fire trucks and fire fighters equipped with PDAs or laptops have to exchange large amounts of data over the ad-hoc network. Some of these devices, primarily UAVs and fire trucks, also serve as gateways to the WSN and provide the context information to the other MANET devices. This results in a number of challenges that have to be addressed by the WSN, such as highly mobile multi-sinks (speeds vary from that of a typical pedestrial to that of a flying UAV). Additionally, the deployed sensor network might be disconnected due to holes in the deployment, sink mobility, destruction of sensor nodes by fire or node failures due to energy depletion.

The information of the WSN has to be annotated with location information to be of use in this scenario. Therefore, we assume that all sensor nodes know their positions, which can be assigned by a UAV directly prior to the deployment. This makes it possible to query a part of the sensor network by specifying an area of interest.

In this chapter we concentrate on providing efficient access of MANET devices to context information provided by a WSN with the help of gateway nodes. The reduction of the message overhead and the overall energy consumption of the WSN is the foremost goal as well as the support for gateway and sensor node mobility. The following challenges are considered: 1) scoping of query dissemination to areas of interest; 2) efficient network reconfiguration due to topology changes; 3) efficient handling of node and especially sink mobility.

We solve the listed challenges by defining convex groups that encapsulate the coverage information of the WSN. The convex group of each subtree is calculated on-the-fly along the routing tree to the nearest sink. Moreover, changes in the routing tree, e.g. due to node mobility, require recalculation only of a limited number of groups and, therefore, impact only a limited part of the network. Additionally, it is possible to limit the space complexity of convex groups to a constant value by lossy compression, which can reduce the message overhead but does not impair the correctness of query dissemination.

We discuss several alternative approaches and argue that convex groups are a low-cost and practical abstraction which enables efficient cooperation of multiple sinks. We propose a new approach that leverages position information to optimize cooperation among gateways in multi-sink scenarios by hierarchical spatial scoping. This enables efficient query dissemination and supports node and sink mobility, taking position inaccuracy, topology changes and poor link quality into account.

6.2 Related Work

There are a number of related approaches in the area of efficient partitioning of a sensor network among multiple sinks, boundary or contour approximation of each partition and optimization techniques for data acquisition.

6.2.1 Network Partitioning

Multi-sink partitioning: Many real-world applications consider the problem of multi-sink routing in sensor networks. However, little research has been conducted in this area [DD05]. The simplest possible solution is for each sink to disseminate messages to the whole network. However, this approach is redundant and the per node overhead increases linearly with the number of sinks [DFES04]. The algorithm presented in [DFE04, DFES04] describes Voronoi scoping – a distributed algorithm to constrain the dissemination of messages from different sinks by introducing Voronoi clusters. Every node belongs to the Voronoi cluster of the closest sink, where "closest" depends on the underlying distance metric. In [DD05] the authors generalize Voronoi scoping by introducing the so-called Logical Graph Model, where multiple sinks are seen as a single logical sink. The constructed graph allows for easy adaptation of algorithms that have been designed for single sinks to multi-sink data acquisition. Other related scoping techniques include TTL scoping and geographic scoping that consider partitioning of sensor network based on the number of hops a message is allowed to travel in the network (time-to-live) and the Euclidian distance to the nearest sink respectively.

The approach presented in this chapter can use any of the discussed scoping metrics or any other tree-forming routing metric to partition the network. However, our approach additionally leverages the knowledge of node positions to enable efficient querying of subregions of the sensor network. Therefore, the hierarchical convex groups allow for extended scoping that is necessary to route the data between the closest sink and the subregion of interest.

Clustering: Clustering of a sensor network [HCB00, AY07, BC03, YS07, GMKR07] is very popular compared to plain routing and reduces the number of generated messages by allowing for data aggregation at cluster heads [MFHH02]. Known approaches consider clustering of sensor nodes based on network connectivity graph or available energy resources [HCB00, AY07, BC03], spatial [YS07] or semantic [GMKR07] data correlations. A key difference of the present algorithm to these clustering approaces is that they dynamically elect cluster head nodes at runtime, whereas here the sinks are determined a priori and the algorithm itself is not responsible for selecting which node can be a cluster head or a sink.

6.2.2 Boundary or Contour Approximation

Boundary recognition: Boundary recognition and hole detection gained popularity in sensor networks in the last few years [FK06b, WGM06, KFPF06, HHMS03, BGHS06]. There are several approaches [FK06b, WGM06, KFPF06] that recognize network boundaries when node coordinates are not available but instead use the connectivity graph of the network and assumptions on its embedding. The algorithms described in [FK06b, WGM06] are based on the assumption that the shortest path provides a good approximation of the distance between the nodes and, therefore, require quite high node density to provide reasonable results. In [KFPF06] the algorithm provides approximation of the network boundaries by recognizing subgraphs that provide guarantees for a set of nodes to lie inside of the network for any d-QUDG embedding of the network connectivity graph for $d \geq \frac{\sqrt{2}}{2}$.

Contour approximation: Even when sensor node positions are known, the problem of representing complex geometric shapes using limited memory is fundamental in many sensor network applications, e.g. producing contour maps based on sensor readings [Est03] or vehicle tracking [LWHS02]. Therefore, the contour approximation problem has often been considered in the literature [HHMS03, BGHS06]. The algorithm proposed in [HHMS03] provides the approximation of a contour by axis-aligned bounding boxes. The main disadvantage of this approach is that this approximation imposes an axis-dependence where none is required [BGHS06]. Moreover, such approximation is very inaccurate. The algorithm presented in [BGHS06] approximates the contour with a not necessarily convex k-vertex polygon by the so-called Adaptive Group Merge algorithm.

These approaches are used to either detect or describe geometric properties, whereas convex grouping uses the hierarchical inclusion of areas to optimize information dissemination in the network.

6.2.3 Data Acquisition

Query dissemination: Querying is typically done through techniques such as flooding [IGE00], minimum broadcast tree algorithms [Lia02, WNE02], or probabilistic algorithms such as gossiping [KK02]. The approach presented in this chapter differs from these approaches by using the knowledge of the sensor node coordinates to scope query dissemination messages with convex groups. Moreover, convex groups allow to limit the flooding between the sink and the destination subregion and, therefore, to prolong network lifetime.

Data collection: In both single- and multi-sink scenarios, the collection of sensor data from data sources to a sink is usually done by means of a routing tree [CABM05, SML+06]. In [MFHH02] it was shown that in-network data aggregation along the routing tree considerably reduces energy consumption of the sensor network and prolongs network lifetime. A number of approaches have been proposed in this field [HHMS03, MFHH02, SBAS04]. The focus of these works is on numerical summaries over sensor data, such as maximum, average, count or median. The main focus of the approach presented in this chapter is set on the spatial summary.

Since we assume that all nodes know their coordinates, we also have to consider geographic routing approaches like GPSR [KK00] in the context of the gateway cooperation problem. However, since these approaches do not tackle specifically the problem of tree-based collection and dissemination, they do not provide an efficient solution. Additionally, the protocols might either fail on random network topologies or are very complex and require the computation of a planar subgraph of the underlying connectivity graph. This works for the unit disk graph model but the existing planarization techniques fail for realistic, non-ideal radio propagation patterns [KGKS05]. Moreover, geographic routing might fail if coordinate information is inaccurate. The convex groups approach overcomes these limitations, while still providing support for sensor node and sink mobility, and the algorithm is simpler compared to geographic routing.

6.3 Motivation

In the following subsections we describe the scenario that motivates the need for gateway cooperation when sensor nodes know their coordinates. Then, we discuss the possible approaches for gateway cooperation and describe the advantages of the concept of convex groups.

6.3.1 Fire Fighting Scenario

The AWARE project (cf. Section 2.3) has been established to study the potential for self-organising and collaborative sensor networks. In particular, the cooperation of a wireless ground sensor network comprising static as well mobile devices with unmanned aerial vehicles (UAVs). In this scenario it is essential to establish an efficient communication and cooperation platform that is able to self-organize, adapt to changes and provide support in case of accidents.

The primary application of the AWARE platform is a fire fighting scenario in which the UAVs must trigger an alarm if a fire is detected and start to deploy the sensor nodes which measure temperature, gas level and other environmental data in order to transmit this information to the fire fighters and mission coordinators.

The described scenario involves two rather different communication standards: UAVs and PDAs communicate over IEEE 802.11.g in ad-hoc mode and sensor networks usually use low power and cheap tranceivers for example employing the IEEE 802.15.4 standard. Moreover, the devices in the high and in the low bandwidth parts of the AWARE network tend to use different communication paradigms: address centric and data centric respectively. Therefore, there is a strong need for gateway devices equipped with both communication interfaces to cooperate efficiently in order to achieve the goals of AWARE.

6.3.2 Gateway Cooperation

The first problem to solve is to define the areas every mobile gateway is responsible for in order to avoid that all queries have to be forwarded to all sensor networks via all gateways. There are two groups of approaches to define such areas: *top-down* and *bottom-up*.

Top-down approaches leave the network partitioning task to sink nodes. As soon as sink nodes define their areas of responsibility, the sensor nodes are notified by every sink providing a description of the area. Every sensor node then easily decides on the area it belongs to. For example, the sink nodes might partition the target area by Voronoi tessellation to define their areas of responsibility. The main disadvantage of this group of approaches is that the partitioning does not take into account possible absence of connectivity in a sensor network within each partition. This happens due to non-uniform deployment of nodes in certain areas, routing holes due to environment characteristics, unstable and asymmetric communication links between the nodes and node mobility. Therefore, top-down area partitioning often causes unreachable nodes in the network.

The other group of approaches for the definition of the areas of responsibility for every sink node is based on the cooperation of sensor nodes within the network. These are *bottom-up* approaches. Based on the own position each sensor node selects the nearest gateway and sends a notification specifying its position. This group of approaches is very attractive because it is possible to preserve the reachability between a sensor node and the sink it belongs to. The approach proposed in this chapter belongs to this group of approaches.

In the next section we give the definition of convex groups and describe the supporting algorithms.

6.4 Distributed Convex Groups

6.4.1 Establishing Convex Groups

Convex Groups are extremely useful in mobile multi-sink scenarios and help to approximate the areas of responsibility for every sink. This allows more efficient querying of a part of a sensor network while avoiding unnecessary flooding of the complete network with query messages. Moreover, convex groups can be used for event detection when aggregating the event descriptions from several sensor nodes and simultaneously approximating the event area.

As in the previous chapter, a sensor network is modelled as an undirected graph $G = (V, E)$ with an edge between any two nodes that can communicate with each other (Terminology is summarized in Section 6.8). We propose the idea of constructing hierarchical *Convex Groups* along the routing tree in order to abstract the target area. Consider a set of s nodes $V_{[s]} \subseteq V$. We say that a polygon $P_{[n]}$ defines a *convex group* over $V_{[s]}$ if it is a convex polygon of n vertices, that covers all s nodes in $V_{[s]}$. If there is no limit on the number of vertices the polygon $P_{[n]}$ may comprise, then the minimum $P_{[n]}$ coincides with the convex hull $C_{[m]}$ built over the set of nodes $V_{[s]}$ ($n = m$). Moreover, it is possible to define a *compressed* polygon $P_{[n']}$ which contains the convex hull but comprises less vertices ($n' < m$) and which has, therefore, a larger area. This polygon might consist of vertices with coordinates different from any of the actual sensor nodes. Compression may be used to limit the amount of storage needed for polygon descriptions. In the evaluation section of this chapter we will show that the constructed convex groups are a good approximation of the covered area.

The operator $g : V_{[s]} \rightarrow P_{[n]}$ constructs a convex group $P_{[n]}$ on the set of nodes $V_{[s]}$ without compression. The construction of *Convex Groups* along the routing tree corresponds to the divide and conquer approach of constructing a convex hull. However, the merge step of this approach assumes that the convex polygons to be merged are disjoint. This cannot be guaranteed when convex groups are built over a routing tree structure Fig.6.1) in contrast to an explicit divide operation where all vertices are sorted based on their x-coordinates and the resulting sequence is cut in halves. Therefore, we adopted the Rotating Calipers approach described in [Sha78, Tou83] to solve this problem. We need the following definitions to describe this algorithm.

Directed line of support A directed line of support l for a polygon is a line intersecting it such that the interior of the polygon lies completely to one side of l. This is comparable to a tangent line of a circle. The direction of the line of support is relevant when requiring parallel lines of support.

Co-podal pair A co-podal pair for two convex polygons P and Q is a pair of points $p \in P, q \in Q$ such that parallel directed lines of support $line_p$ and $line_q$ through p and q respectively exist and P lies on the same side of $line_p$ as Q of $line_q$.

Bridge A bridge is used to connect vertices of two convex polygons to form the convex hull of both. Together with the convex chains of each polygon they form a new convex polygon. If two disjoint polygons are merged, then exactly two bridges are needed. If the polygons overlap, the number of bridges may at most equal the minimum number of vertices of the existing polygons.

The Rotating Calipers are used to find the bridges between two convex possibly overlapping polygons. The following result is the foundation for this algorithm: Given two convex polygons $P_{[n]} = \{p_0, ..., p_{n-1}\}$ and $Q_{[w]} = \{q_0, ..., q_{w-1}\}$, a pair of points (p_i, q_j) form a bridge between $P_{[n]}$ and $Q_{[w]}$

if, and only if:

1. (p_i, q_j) form a *co-podal pair*.

2. p_{i-1}, p_{i+1}, q_{j-1}, q_{j+1}, lie on the same side of the line joining (p_i, q_j).

Assuming the vertices of the polygon are in clockwise order, the algorithm involves the following steps.

Step 1 For P and Q, compute the vertices p_i, q_j with the maximum y-coordinate (if necessary, compare x-coordinates to ensure uniqueness)

Step 2 Construct two directed horizontal lines of support through p_i and q_j such that the polygons lie to the right of the respective lines. This results in a co-podal pair.

Step 3 A new co-podal pair is found by rotating both lines of support clockwise until at least one line coincides with an edge. Three co-podal pairs are found if the edges are parallel.

Step 4 For each co-podal pair (p_i, q_j) found, check if all neighbors $(p_{i-1}, p_{i+1}, q_{j-1}, q_{j+1})$ lie on the same side of the line through p_i, q_j. If this is true, the segment between p_i and q_j is a bridge.

Step 5 Steps 3 and 4 are repeated until the directed lines of support reach their original horizontal position.

Step 6 The convex hull is constructed by joining the determined bridges with the necessary convex chains of the original polygons connecting consecutive bridges.

This algorithm has two major advantages: it involves no backtracking and even more importantly for our approach, it does not require that the polygons do not intersect. The algorithm has linear time complexity. The convex hull algorithm using Rotating Calipers merge for possibly intersecting polygons runs in $O(n \log n)$ time and requires $O(n)$ space.

For the distributed construction of *Convex Groups* along the routing tree, every parent node receives the convex group information from all its children and merges them together with the addition of the parent node itself. In such a way a new composite convex group is constructed which is forwarded further. This allows the construction of a hierarchy of convex groups. The distributed procedure requires $O(1)$ messages per sensor node, $O(dm)$ space and runs in $O(dm)$ time, where d is the maximum node degree in the network and m is the maximum number of nodes in a convex polygon.

Using the structure of the routing tree has a number of advantages. First, the constructed convex groups encapsulate connectivity information which

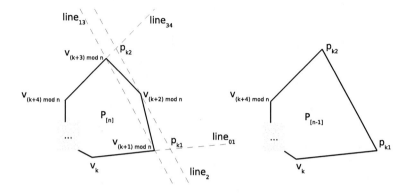

Figure 6.1: Compression step: $c : P_{[n]} \to P_{[n-1]}$

is very important for the wireless sensor nodes. Moreover, depending on the routing metric used every node belongs to the convex group of the best parent in the sense of link quality, number of required transmissions, energy consumption or delay. Second, the routing tree structure provides the possibility to define a natural hierarchy over the convex groups. In the evaluation section we will argue that this hierarchy is extremely important in case of node mobility and allows for efficient routing and data dissemination in mobile scenarios.

6.4.2 Compression of Convex Groups

Since the number of bytes to be transmitted with one message is very limited (usually 29 bytes in TinyOS messages) and main memory is scarce on sensor network devices, it might be necessary to limit the number of vertices that approximate a convex group accepting a small loss of quality. To achieve this, the algorithm transforms the merged polygon $P_{[n]}$ in another one $P_{[k]}$ ($k < n$) if the number of vertices in a merged polygon exceeds a predefined threshold. We refer to this step as *compression*.

Consider a convex polygon $P_{[n]}$ which is a convex hull of n vertices over the set of vertices $V_{[s]}$ on the plane. We define a compression operator $c : P_{[n]} \to P_{[n-1]}$ which converts the given convex polygon of n vertices into a convex polygon of $n - 1$ vertices which contains $P_{[n]}$. The Algorithm 5 describes the compression procedure performed by the operator c (also see Fig. 6.1).

The operator c has the following properties:

- **Convexity:** $c(P_{[n]})$ is convex if $P_{[n]}$ is convex
- **Inclusion:** $P_{[n]} \subseteq c(P_{[n]})$
- **Iterative applicability:** $P_{[n]} = c(P_{[n+1]})$

These properties allow us to iteratively apply the compression operator at each step along the routing tree in order to limit the number of vertices in the convex groups. The computational complexity of one iteration step is $O(n)$ for an input polygon $P_{[n]}$.

Procedure Compress $P_{[n]}$

```
/* Converts convex P[n], n > 3 to convex P[n-1] ⊇ P[n]          */
```
$S \leftarrow \infty, m, p_1, p_2$
for *in* $P_{[n]}$: $k = 0..n-1$ **do**
    $line_{01} \leftarrow line(v_k, v_{(k+1) \bmod n})$
    $line_{34} \leftarrow line(v_{(k+3) \bmod n}, v_{(k+4) \bmod n})$
    $line_{13} \leftarrow line(v_{(k+1) \bmod n}, v_{(k+3) \bmod n})$
    $line_2 \leftarrow line(v_{(k+2) \bmod n}) \parallel line_{13}$
    $p_{k1} \leftarrow line_{01} \cap line_2$
    $p_{k2} \leftarrow line_{34} \cap line_2$
    $S_k \leftarrow area_\Delta(v_{(k+1) \bmod n}, p_{k1}, v_{(k+2) \bmod n}) +$
    $area_\Delta(v_{(k+2) \bmod n}, p_{k2}, v_{(k+3) \bmod n})$
    if $S > S_k$ **then**
       $S \leftarrow S_k,\ p_1 \leftarrow p_{k1},\ p_2 \leftarrow p_{k2},\ m \leftarrow k$
    endif
endfor
in $P_{[n]}$: $v_{(m+1) \bmod n} \leftarrow p_1$
in $P_{[n]}$: $v_{(m+3) \bmod n} \leftarrow p_2$
$P_{[n-1]} \leftarrow$ *in* $P_{[n]}$: remove $v_{(m+2) \bmod n}$
return $P_{[n-1]}$

6.4.3 Properties of Convex Groups

The *Convex Groups* have the following properties:

Scoping: Every convex group describes a subregion on the monitoring area. This subregion is the scope of the convex group. When a query concerning this subregion is disseminated by the closest sink node, only the convex groups with higher hierarchy level that include this region are affected (*down-streaming*). The response to the query is propagated along the reverse path to the closest sink (*up-streaming*). Additionally, convex groups built along the routing tree allow more efficient in-network data aggregation. The aggregation function might decide to merge the scopes into a larger convex group or forward the data of both convex groups separately.

Scalability: The introduction of multiple sinks increases the scalability of sensor networks [DFES04]. Additionally, the presented convex group scoping provides a practical method for specifying subregions of any size and due to compression provides a very scalable abstraction.

Maintenance overhead: We have to distinguish between the case when a parent node knows all of its children and when each node knows only its parent. In the first case, it is possible that a parent waits for the information of all its children and only then forwards the complete convex group to its parent. This results in a minimum message overhead for the transmission of convex group information but requires not only more memory on the parent node but also a larger number of messages for the construction and maintenance of the routing tree itself. This overhead is more acceptable if this information is not only used for the convex group construction but also for other parts of the system. When a node only knows its parent but not its children, a heuristic must be used to determine the delay until the convex group is transmitted to the parent. This may result in a larger number of update messages. However, even in the worst case, the network wide number of messages is in $O(hl)$ where h is the maximum depth of the routing tree and l is the number of leaf nodes.

The maintenance of *Convex Groups* requires every parent node to store the vertices of its current convex group, which are a few bytes of memory. If support for node mobility is required, every parent node additionally has to store the convex groups of its children in order to recalculate its convex group without having to request this information for every update it receives.

Mobility: We distinguish sink and sensor node mobility. If a sensor node changes its position, the changes are propagated along the tree only as far as the convex groups are affected. Mobile sinks have a greater influence on the sensor network topology due to more significant changes in the routing tree structure. However, as it is shown in the evaluation section of this chapter, even in this case the number of update messages in the network is reduced by the *Convex Groups* approach.

Reachability: The algorithm guarantees that a query is disseminated to all nodes that are in its scope. This is in contrast to top-down approaches, e.g. a Voronoi tessellation of the sensor network between multiple sinks, which cannot guarantee reachability due to lack of knowledge about the connectivity of the network.

Adaptation: The compression parameter k can be adapted based on different requirements or system characteristics.

Available memory and bandwidth: The amount of memory required as well as the amount of data that has to be transmitted is directly related to k. By limiting k the linear space complexity can be reduced to a constant one.

Position accuracy: As is shown in the evaluation, lower values of k are better suited for inaccurate positions, since the area of a convex group is over-estimated by compression and thus the number of nodes falsely considered to be outside of a convex group is reduced.

Link quality: Closely related to the previous point and also illustrated in the evaluation is the suitability of lower values of k in case of low link quality. The over-estimation of areas due to compression reduces the error incurred by packet losses.

Network density: If a parent stores the convex groups of all its children, which is necessary for the support of mobility, the amount of memory required is kd (d is the network density). Therefore, to reduce the memory overhead in case of high network densities lower values of k are advisable.

6.5 Evaluation

We evaluated our approach by exhaustive simulations varying the number of sensor nodes and the number of sinks. The nodes are deployed in a rectangular region of 1200 m × 800 m. Every sensor node has a transmission range of 120 m, which is typical for outdoor scenarios [BI05]. All tests used a uniform distribution of the sensor nodes in the deployment area. We used a Random Waypoint movement model [SHB+03] provided by the CANU Mobility Simulation Environment[1] to simulate sensor node and sink mobility. Moreover, we used input parameter settings for user mobility in rescue mission as described in [SHB+03]. The typical speeds for UAVs (40-60 km/h) are taken form the AWARE specification document and were used in the real-world AWARE experiments in March 2008 in Utrera, Spain. The mobility simulations lasted 30 simulation minutes each with update step of 10 seconds.

---

[1]http://canu.informatik.uni-stuttgart.de/mobisim/

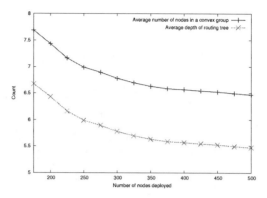

Figure 6.2: Average convex group size and routing tree depth

The number of convex groups is always equal to the number of deployed nodes, because every node is the head of the convex group that comprises the convex groups of its descendants in the routing tree. In Fig. 6.2 we evaluated the average number of sensor nodes in a convex group and the average depth of the constructed routing tree. We used the Shortest Path First routing metric [CACM03] to build a routing tree. However, the *Convex Groups* are not limited to a certain routing metric and can be used in combination with any routing metric, e.g. [SML+06, CABM05]. The average values are calculated over 20 deployments for a fixed number of sensor nodes.

As it was previously discussed, the inclusion property holds for convex groups. Therefore, it is interesting to evaluate the accumulated error of computing convex groups with and without compression. In Fig. 6.3 we show the average and maximum error obtained for different values of the compression parameter k. Here we varied the number of nodes in the deployment from 150 to 300 and simulated a total of 200 topologies. The compression error decreases exponentially with increasing k. Therefore, the value of k can be chosen based on user requirements on the quality of convex grouping.

The only possibility to assign exact positions to sensor nodes is to do it manually. All other techniques like GPS receivers, node localization algorithms [LR03] or assignment of node positions by a UAV in the deployment phase result in inaccuracy of node positions. In Fig. 6.4 we evaluate the influence of position inaccuracy on the quality of convex grouping. The results show, that the use of compression allows to hide inaccuracy of node

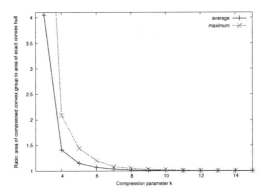

Figure 6.3: Loss of accuracy due to the compression of convex groups

positions to some extent. We used 200 deployments of 200 nodes for this evaluation. The positioning error is uniformly distributed within the given error radius. We evaluated the number of sensor nodes that due to position inaccuracy do not belong to the convex groups they must belong to. The positioning error of 40% (normalized by the transmission range) results in 16% of nodes being outside of their corresponding convex groups on average.

Packet losses are unavoidable in sensor networks and make many algorithms hardly applicable to real-world deployments. Therefore, we evaluated the influence of losses of packets containing convex group information on the correctness of the convex groups. We count the number of nodes that lie outside of a convex group they should belong to. In Fig. 6.5 we plot the percentage of such nodes in the network versus the link packet loss rate for the case when each packet is sent once $(r = 0)$ and for the case when one retransmission per link in case of transmission failure $(r = 1)$ is used for convex grouping information. If a packet is lost on one of the wireless links, the information of the whole subtree is lost. The average depth of the routing tree is plotted in Fig. 6.2. With no retransmissions the convex grouping error reaches 35% with link packet losses of 20%, however, the use of one retransmission reduces this error to 5.5% on average. The use of compression slightly reduces the convex grouping error as well. The average values in Fig.6.5 are built over 10 topologies of 300 nodes.

The application of convex grouping allows to reduce the number of broadcasts required to disseminate query information. We assume that queries refer to a certain subregion of the deployment area – the area of interest.

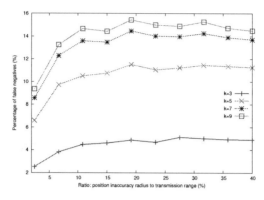

Figure 6.4: Impact of position inaccuracy on convex grouping

We use square areas with different sizes for the simulation. In Fig. 6.6 we show the dependency between the size of the subregion addressed by the query (relative to the overall deployment area) and the number of nodes that broadcast the query to their dependent convex groups. A low value of the compression parameter k slightly increases the number of nodes that need to broadcast the query due to the inaccuracy of the convex hull approximation resulted by compression. This evaluation result shows the average of 20 deployments of 250 sensor nodes for every point in the figure. This graph shows, that for both single and multiple-sink scenarios the application of convex groups allows to reduce the number of message broadcasts for query dissemination considerably. Compared to flooding, which is usually used for query dissemination, e.g. in TinyDB [MFHH05, MFHH02], and requires all sensor nodes to broadcast a message, convex groups reduce the number of broadcasts considerably and, therefore, prolong the lifetime of the sensor network.

Many algorithms for sensor networks concentrate on static or low mobility applications. However, in many rescue and civil security/disaster management scenarios like AWARE, it is very important to take node mobility into account and to use algorithms that provide additional support for node mobility. We distinguish two types of mobility: sensor node mobility and sink mobility. In Fig. 6.7, we plot the dependence between the number of mobile sensor nodes that represent the fire fighters moving according to the Random Waypoint model with parameters as suggested in [SHB+03] for rescue missions. As can be seen from the graph, we experimented with 2 to 20 mobile sensor nodes out of 250 which results in up to 25% of changes in convex

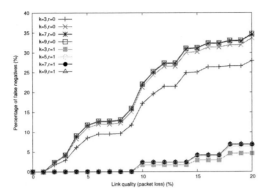

Figure 6.5: Impact of packet loss on convex grouping

groups. Notice, that lower values of the compression parameter k result in a slightly higher percentage of group changes. The reason for this behaviour lies in the distributed computation of the convex hulls and the application of the compression step at each level. Each convex group is composed of two or more subgroups with the exception of leaf nodes. If a node moves within a composite convex group, it does not influence it, since it is not part of the boundary. However, if compression is applied, the movement of the node may influence the position of vertices which are on the boundary of a subgroup and of the composite group. Therefore, even nodes traveling inside of a convex group might change the boundary of this convex group.

Finally, we explored the influence of sink mobility on the algorithm. In Fig. 6.8 we consider the case when 1 or 3 sinks move with different speeds according to the Random Waypoint model. We varied the speeds of mobile sinks from the range of a typical pedestrian (4-6 km/h) to a flying UAV (40-60 km/h) and calculated the average number of convex group changes per update interval (10 sec). Lower values of k result in a slightly higher number of group changes for the same reason as explained above.

The evaluation results of scenarios involving mobile devices show the advantage of using the hierarchy of the routing tree. Only changes that affect a convex group are forwarded. Since the scope of the convex group increases along the routing tree, the probability that a change on a lower level influences a convex group decreases and thus a change does not usually propagate to the sink. This is in contrast to simple approaches where all node positions are forwarded indiscriminately and only the sink uses this information

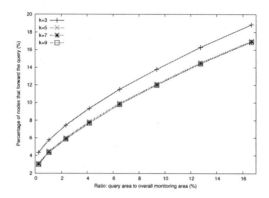

Figure 6.6: Efficiency of query dissemination

to compute the area of its responsibility. The worst case message complexity of convex grouping occurs when all nodes move in such a way that all convex groups have to be updated. Only in this case is the message overhead comparable to the message complexity always required by the described related approaches. However, convex groups perform much better in the average case.

6.6 Structure Analysis

This section provides an overview and a comparison of the *Convex Group* and the *Voronoi Partitioning* algorithms in terms of the partitioning structures they build. The algorithm properties are summarized in Table 6.1.

Algorithms that solve the problem of network partitioning rely on the knowledge of sensor node coordinates. Node coordinates are a reliable and stable characteristic. Therefore, stability, convergence and a low reconfiguration overhead are guaranteed for both partitioning algorithms developed in this thesis.

Partitioning algorithms build global structures. These algorithms can be considered scalable since they generate only a low construction and maintenance overhead. However, there does not seem to exist a scalable solution for the assignment of geographic coordinates to nodes. Therefore, coordinate assignment algorithms only hide the lack of scalability and the overhead of algorithms calculating a partitioning of the network.

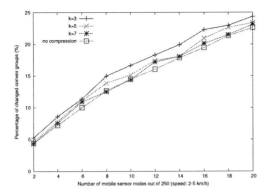

Figure 6.7: Impact of node mobility on maintenance overhead of convex grouping

The bottom-up partitioning solution, *Convex Groups*, provides a better support for limited node and sink mobility compared to the *Voronoi Partitioning* algorithm as has been shown in this chapter. However, the node localization system used by the algorithm has to be able to handle this mobility. Moreover, partitioning structures do not decay over time and are, therefore, static but evolving.

The *Convex Groups* partitioning algorithm solves the problem in a bottom-up manner while *Voronoi Partitioning* uses a top-down approach. As argued in this chapter, the bottom-up approach better supports sink and node mo-

Property	Convex Groups	Voronoi Partitioning
Stab./Reconfig	+	+
Convergence	+	+
Param./Adapt	+	-
Temp./Static	S	S
Coordinates	+	+
Mobility	+	+
Scalability	+	+
Overhead	low	low
Top-down/Bottom-up	BU	TD

Table 6.1: Classification of partitioning algorithms and obtained structures

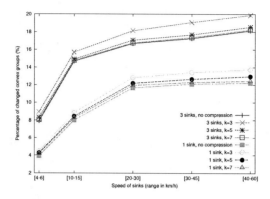

Figure 6.8: Impact of sink mobility on maintenance overhead of convex grouping

bility and is more stable compared to its alternative.

The *Convex Groups* algorithm is parameterized with the underlying routing algorithm. This means that different routing trees result in different multi-sink partitions. Such parameterization leads to an efficient combination of these algorithms.

6.7 Summary

In this chapter we have presented the notion of *Convex Groups* for multi-sink wireless sensor networks – groups of nodes included in a convex region in the deployment area. Every node stores the spatial summary of the region it is responsible for. We have provided algorithms that allow to efficiently build convex groups and support lossy compression to reduce the amount of spatial summary information and thereby the message complexity. This makes *Convex Groups* a powerful abstraction that allows for efficient querying of a sensor network and supports both sensor node and sink mobility, which is important for rescue missions and civil security operations.

6.8 Appendix: Terminology

$G(V, E)$	Undirected graph that models a sensor network
V	Set of nodes in a sensor network
E	Set of communication links between nodes
$V_{[s]} \subseteq V$	Subset of s sensor nodes
$P_{[n]}$	Convex polygon of n vertices
$C_{[m]}$	Convex hull
$g : V_{[s]} \to P_{[n]}$	Convex group construction operator
$c : P_{[n]} \to P_{[n-1]}$	Compression operator
k	Compression parameter
l	Directed line of support
d	Maximum node degree in the network
m	Maximum number of nodes in a convex polygon
$line_{xy}$	Line through nodes x and y
$line_z$	Line through node z
r	Number of retransmissions

6 Convex Groups

7 Conclusions and Outlook

In this thesis, we have investigated the concept of structures in wireless sensor networks. We have motivated why structures are important and why the performance of structuring algorithms is critical to the success of wireless sensor networks. With the help of several example applications, we have extracted important properties of structures and requirements to structures and structuring algorithms.

Based on a comprehensive understanding of structures in wireless sensor networks, we have developed and thoroughly analyzed four different algorithms for structuring of wireless sensor networks. Three of them deal with generating structures that support applications running on sensor nodes and result in the formation of routing tree structures, dynamic grouping of nodes and partitioning of nodes in the network. The fourth approach discussed in this thesis provides an efficient mechanism for recognition of the network boundary and the boundaries of holes in the network. This approach works on a different but equally important structuring problem: the detection and extraction of information about structures which are naturally present within wireless sensor networks. In addition to the individual contributions to these four specific research areas, our analysis also proves that structuring is both important and omnipresent in wireless sensor networks. By carefully designing these mechanisms, we were able to significantly improve the performance, quality of the results and scalability of the resulting systems.

7.1 Conclusions

The formation of structures is an important part of self-organization of wireless sensor nodes and a precondition for their successful cooperation. However, structuring algorithms need to be carefully designed in order to take advantage of the specific properties of the structure, sensor network model and specifics of the underlying network algorithms.

Our analysis of different structures and sensor network applications has revealed a set of fundamental properties of efficient structuring algorithms in wireless sensor networks that need to be considered in the algorithm design.

Firstly, if the algorithm uses only local knowledge, then self-similar structures are created. Examples of self-similar structures are routing trees and partitioning structures generated by the Convex Groups approach. Boundary recognition also works with local knowledge but does not result in a self-similar structures since this approach extracts structural information rather than generates structures.

Secondly, building structures using global knowledge generates a higher construction and maintenance overhead which is usually inevitable for global structures. For example, ST-grouping with the backtracking approach has a high worst case construction overhead that grows with the size of the network. In general, introducing structures in wireless sensor networks usually supports the formation of scalable systems.

Thirdly, a fast and provable convergence of the structuring algorithm is essential to avoid oscillations within the structure. We have shown that all four structuring approaches presented in this thesis reliably converge.

Fourthly, an inherent trade-off exists between the stability of a structure and its reconfiguration. A compromise between these conflicting goals must be found based on the application requirements and the properties of a target environment. Among our four structuring approaches, this trade-off is often considered important for the routing tree structure: depending on how the metric is defined, it either tends to stabilize well but react slowly to topology changes or it quickly adapts to changes in the environment while it is less stable.

Fifthly, the parameterization and the adaptation are important properties of structuring algorithms, because the specifics of the environment are often unknown prior to the deployment of the sensor network and might also change over time. Our routing approach, the boundary recognition algorithm and the partitioning algorithm are all parameterizable which allows for application specific applications.

Structuring algorithms are constructed based on a model describing the real world. A more detailed model allows a better tailored construction of the structuring algorithm. However, there are two orthogonal flows to consider: incorporation of additional knowledge allows to improve the structure but might also lead to model overfitting. For example, the knowledge of node coordinates allows to approximate the network boundaries considerably better and with less effort. However, a generalization of the network model to cover a larger spectrum of application scenarios leads to a higher complexity of the algorithms and to less tractable resulting structures.

The structuring algorithm often determines the properties of the resulting structure. For example, the behavior of a link quality estimator heavily influences the reconfiguration speed and the overall construction time of a routing tree. Another example is routing which is used for partitioning the network. Instabilities of the routing algorithm also negatively affect the stability of the partitioning algorithm that works on top of it. This is another strong argument in favor of cross-layer design in wireless sensor networks.

Finally, the application scenario of a sensor network determines the importance of structures and the types of structures used. Structures play an important role in static sensor network deployments and networks with limited node mobility. Mobility and the reaction to events are often the reasons for choosing algorithms that generate temporary structures rather than those with static structures.

7.2 Outlook

By examining structures and structuring algorithms, this thesis has covered an important aspect of self-organization in wireless sensor networks. However, the problem of self-organization itself as well as the properties of the self-organization algorithms and the results of this organization remain important research topics.

We envision growing interest of the wireless sensor network community in structures when designing and analyzing algorithms, protocols and sensor network applications.

Firstly, self-similar structures and properties of the algorithms generating such structures should be further investigated. The application of this principle allows to considerably reduce message, computational and storage complexities of algorithms that construct global structures, which saves energy and considerably minimizes the overhead for maintaining structures.

Secondly, the concept of structures allows to facilitate cross-layer interactions between different algorithms on the network level. The topic of cross-layer interactions between different software modules on the same node has received much attention in the last years. However, the analysis of structures allows to reason about the unification of structures constructed by different algorithms. Some works on this topic already exist: [MFHH05] uses the same tree structure for routing and aggregation, and [KFPF06] uses information about the network boundary for an efficient load-balancing routing mechanism. We envision further research and formalization of the structure unification operation and investigation of its potential.

Finally, the separation of structure properties from properties of the structuring algorithms allows to better understand a number of algorithm classes. Careful analysis and increased insight into the dependencies, requirements and impact of these properties leads to discovering optimization possibilities in existing algorithms and improves the development of future algorithms.

Bibliography

[ABC⁺03]   Javed Aslam, Zack Butler, Florin Constantin, Valentino Crespi, George Cybenko, and Daniela Rus. Tracking a moving object with a binary sensor network. In *Proceedings of the 1st international conference on Embedded networked sensor systems (SenSys 2003)*, pages 150–161, New York, NY, USA, 2003. ACM.

[AGY04]   James Aspnes, David Goldenberg, and Yang Richard Yang. On the computational complexity of sensor network localization. 3121:32–44, 2004.

[AWA]   Aware project. http://aware-project.net/.

[AY07]   Ameer Ahmed Abbasi and Mohamed Younis. A survey on clustering algorithms for wireless sensor networks. *Computer Communications*, 30, 2007.

[BC03]   Seema Bandyopadhyay and Edward J. Coyle. An energy efficient hierarchical clustering algorithm for wireless sensor networks. In *Proc. of the 22nd Conference of the IEEE Computer and Communications Societies*, 2003.

[BCD⁺05]   Shah Bhatti, James Carlson, Hui Dai, Jing Deng, Jeff Rose, Anmol Sheth, Brian Shucker, Charles Gruenwald, Adam Torgerson, and Richard Han. MANTIS OS: An embedded multithreaded operating system for wireless micro sensor platforms. *Mobile Network Applications*, 10(4):563–579, 2005.

[BE02]   David Braginsky and Deborah Estrin. Rumor routing algorthim for sensor networks. In *Proceedings of the 1st ACM international workshop on Wireless sensor networks and applications (WSNA 2002)*, pages 22–31, New York, NY, USA, 2002. ACM.

[BGHS06]   Chiranjeeb Buragohain, Sorabh Gandhi, John Hershberger, and Subhash Suri. Contour approximation in sensor networks. In *Proc. of the Inter. Conf. on Distributed Computing in Sensor Systems (DCOSS 2006)*, 2006.

[BGJ05] Jehoshua Bruck, Jie Gao, and Anxiao Andrew Jiang. MAP: Medial axis based geometric routing in sensor networks. In *Proc. of the 11th Int. Conf. on Mobile Computing and Networking (MobiCom 2005)*, 2005.

[BHSW07] Rainer Baumann, Simon Heimlicher, Mario Strasser, and Andreas Weibel. A survey on routing metrics. TIK Report 262, ETH Zürich, 2007.

[BI05] Michael I. Brownfield and Nathaniel J. Davis IV. Symbiotic highway sensor network. *Vehicular Technology Conference*, 4:2701 – 2705, 2005.

[BK98] Heinz Breu and David G. Kirkpatrick. Unit disk graph recognition is NP-hard. *Computational Geometry: Theory and Applications*, 9:3–24, 1998.

[BKM+04] Jan Beutel, Oliver Kasten, Friedemann Mattern, Kay Römer, Frank Siegemund, and Lothar Thiele. Prototyping wireless sensor network applications with BTnodes. In *1st European Workshop on Wireless Sensor Networks (EWSN 2004)*, number 2920 in LNCS, pages 323–338, Berlin, Germany, January 2004. Springer-Verlag.

[BLRS03] Douglas M. Blough, Mauro Leoncini, Giovanni Resta, and Paolo Santi. The k-neigh protocol for symmetric topology control in ad hoc networks. In *Proc. of the 4th Int. Symp. on Mobile Ad Hoc Networking & Computing*, 2003.

[BRI] Sustainable bridges project. `http://www.sustainablebridges.net/`.

[Bru07] Peter Brucker. *Scheduling Algorithms*. Springer; 5th ed. edition (March 12, 2007), 2007.

[BS07] Najet Boughanmi and Ye-Qiong Song. A New Routing Metric for Satisfying Both Energy and Delay Constraints in Wireless Sensor Networks. *Journal of Signal Processing Systems*, 10:137–143, 2007.

[CABM05] Douglas S. J. De Couto, Daniel Aguayo, John Bicket, and Robert Morris. A high-throughput path metric for multi-hop wireless routing. *Journal on Wireless Networks*, 11(4):419–434, 2005.

[CACM03]   Douglas S. J. De Couto, Daniel Aguayo, Benjamin A. Chambers, and Robert Morris. Performance of multihop wireless networks: Shortest path is not enough. *ACM SIGCOMM Computer Communication Review*, 33(1):83–88, 2003.

[DCO04]   Patrick Downey and Rachel Cardell-Oliver. Evaluating the impact of limited resource on the performance of flooding in wireless sensor networks. In *Proceedings of the International Conference on Dependable Systems and Networks (DSN 2004)*, page 785, Washington, DC, USA, 2004. IEEE Computer Society.

[DD05]   Abhimanyu Das and Debojyoti Dutta. Data acquisition in multiple-sink sensor networks. *ACM SIGMOBILE Mobile Computing and Communications Review*, 9:82–85, 2005.

[DFE04]   Henri Dubois-Ferriere and Deborah Estrin. Efficient and practical query scoping in sensor networks. Technical report, 2004.

[DFES04]   Henri Dubois-Ferriere, Deborah Estrin, and Thanos Stathopoulos. Efficient and practical query scoping in sensor networks. In *IEEE Inter. Conf. on Mobile Ad-hoc and Sensor Systems (MASS 2004)*, 2004.

[DGV04]   Adam Dunkels, Bjorn Gronvall, and Thiemo Voigt. Contiki - A lightweight and flexible operating system for tiny networked sensors. In *Proceedings of the 29th Annual IEEE International Conference on Local Computer Networks (LCN 2004)*, pages 455–462, Washington, DC, USA, 2004. IEEE Computer Society.

[Est03]   Deborah Estrin. Embedded networked sensing for environmental monitoring: Applications and challenges. Principles of Mobile Computing, 2003.

[FK06a]   Sandor P. Fekete and Alexander Kröller. Geometry-based reasoning for a large sensor network. In *Proc. of the 22nd Symp. on Computational Geometry*, 2006.

[FK06b]   Stefan Funke and Christian Klein. Hole detection or: "How much geometry hides in connectivity?". In *Proc. of the 22nd Symp. on Computational Geometry*, 2006.

[FKP+04]   Sandor P. Fekete, Alexander Kroeller, Dennis Pfisterer, Stefan Fischer, and Carsten Buschmann. Neighborhood-based topology recognition in sensor networks. In *Proc. of the 1st Int. Workshop on Algorithmic Aspects of Wireless Sensor Networks*, 2004.

[FR05]   Christian Frank and Kay Römer. Algorithms for generic role assignment in wireless sensor networks. In *Proceedings of the 3rd International Conference on Embedded Networked Sensor Systems (SenSys 2005)*, pages 230–242, New York, NY, USA, 2005. ACM.

[FSG02]   Wai Fu Fung, David Sun, and Johannes Gehrke. COUGAR: The network is the database. In *Proceedings of the 2002 ACM SIGMOD international conference on Management of data (SIGMOD 2002)*, pages 621–621, New York, NY, USA, 2002. ACM.

[Fun05]   Stefan Funke. Topological hole detection in wireless sensor networks and its applications. In *Proc. of the Joint Workshop on Foundations of Mobile Computing*, 2005.

[GKW⁺02]   Deepak Ganesan, Bhaskar Krishnamachari, Alec Woo, David Culler, Deborah Estrin, and Stephen Wicker. An empirical study of epidemic algorithms in large scale multihop wireless networks, 2002.

[GMKR07]   Matthias Gauger, Pedro José Marrón, Daniel Kauker, and Kurt Rothermel. Low overhead assignment of symbolic coordinates in sensor networks. In *Proc. of the 1st Inter. Conf. on Wireless Sensor and Actor Networks (WSAN 2007)*, 2007.

[GSH⁺08]   Matthias Gauger, Olga Saukh, Marcus Handte, Pedro José Marrón, Andreas Heydlauff, and Kurt Rothermel. Sensor-based clustering for indoor applications. In *Proceedings of the 5th IEEE Communications Society Conference on Sensor, Mesh and Ad Hoc Communications and Networks (SECON 2008)*, 2008.

[GYHG04]   Omprakash Gnawali, Mark Yarvis, John Heidemann, and Ramesh Govindan. Interaction of Retransmission, Blacklisting, and Routing Metrics for Reliability in Sensor Network Routing. In *Proceedings of the First IEEE Conference on Sensor and Adhoc Communication and Networks*, pages 34–43, Santa Clara, California, USA, October 2004. IEEE.

[GZaDdA⁺05] Peter Gober, Artur Ziviani, Petia Todorova andMarcelo Dias de Amorim, Philipp Huenerberg, and Serge Fdida.

Topology control and localization in wireless ad hoc and sensor networks. *Ad Hoc & Sensor Wireless Networks, OCP Science*, 1(4):301–321, 2005.

[HCB00]   Wendi Rabiner Heinzelman, Anantha Chandrakasan, and Hari Balakrishnan. Energy-efficient communication protocol for wireless microsensor networks. In *Proc. of the 33rd Hawaii International Conference on System Sciences (HICSS 2000)*, 2000.

[HCM05]   Shea R. Kohler E. Han C., Kumar R. Rengaswamy and Srivastava M. Sos: A dynamic operating system for sensor networks. In *Proceedings of the Third International Conference on Mobile Systems, Applications, and Services (Mobisys 2005), Seattle, Washington*, June 2005.

[HHKK04]   Jason Hill, Mike Horton, Ralph Kling, and Lakshman Krishnamurthy. The platforms enabling wireless sensor networks. *Communications of the ACM*, 47(6):41–46, 2004.

[HHMS03]   Joseph M. Hellerstein, Wei Hong, Samuel Madden, and Kyle Stanek. Beyond average: Toward sophisticated sensing with queries. In *Inter. Conf. on Information Processing in Sensor Networks (IPSN 2003)*, 2003.

[HHT02]   Matthias Handy, Marc Haase, and Dirk Timmermann. Low energy adaptive clustering hierarchy with deterministic cluster-head selection. In *In Proc. of the 4th International Workshop on Mobile and Wireless Communications Network*, pages 368–372, 2002.

[IGE00]   Chalermek Intanagonwiwat, Ramesh Govindan, and Deborah Estrin. Directed Diffusion: A Scalable and Robust Communication Paradigm for Sensor Networks. In *Proceedings of the 6th Annual International Conference on Mobile Computing and Networking (MobiCom 2000)*, pages 56–67, New York, NY, USA, 2000. ACM.

[JEN]   Jennic web-site. http://www.jennic.com/.

[JKV05]   D. Janakiram, A V U Phani Kumar, and Adi Mallikarjuna Reddy V. Component oriented middleware for distributed collaboration event detection in wireless sensor networks. In *In Proc. of the 3rd International Workshop on Middleware for Pervasive and Ad-Hoc Computing (MPAC 2005)*, 2005.

Bibliography

[JNRS06]   Lujun Jia, Guevara Noubir, Rajmohan Rajaraman, and Ravi
             Sundaram. GIST: Group-independent spanning tree for data
             aggregation in dense sensor networks. In Phillip B. Gibbons,
             Tarek F. Abdelzaher, James Aspnes, and Ramesh Rao, ed-
             itors, *DCOSS*, volume 4026 of *Lecture Notes in Computer
             Science*, pages 282–304. Springer, 2006.

[JOW+02]   Philo Juang, Hidekazu Oki, Yong Wang, Margaret
             Martonosi, Li Shiuan Peh, and Daniel Rubenstein. Energy-
             efficient computing for wildlife tracking: Design tradeoffs and
             early experiences with zebranet. *SIGARCH Comput. Archit.
             News*, 30(5):96–107, 2002.

[KFPF06]   A. Kröller, S. P. Fekete, D. Pfisterer, and S. Fischer. De-
             terministic boundary recognition and topology extraction for
             large sensor networks. In *Proc. of the 17th Symp. on Discrete
             Algorithms*, 2006.

[KGKS05]   Young-Jin Kim, Ramesh Govindan, Brad Karp, and Scott
             Shenker. On the pitfalls of geographic face routing. In
             *DIALM-POMC '05: Proceedings of the 2005 joint workshop
             on Foundations of mobile computing*, pages 34–43, New York,
             NY, USA, 2005. ACM Press.

[KGKS06]   Young-Jin Kim, Ramesh Govindan, Brad Karp, and Scott
             Shenker. Lazy cross-link removal for geographic routing. In
             *Proceedings of the 4th International Conference on Embedded
             Networked Sensor Systems (SenSys 2006)*, pages 112–124,
             New York, NY, USA, 2006. ACM Press.

[KI04]   Bhaskar Krishnamachari and Sitharama Iyengar. Distributed
             bayesian algorithms for fault-tolerant event region detection
             in wireless sensor networks. *IEEE Transactions on Comput-
             ers*, 53(3):241–250, 2004.

[KK00]   Brad Karp and H. T. Kung. GPSR: Greedy perimeter state-
             less routing for wireless networks. In *Proceedings of the 6th
             annual international conference on Mobile computing and
             networking (MobiCom 2000)*, pages 243–254, New York, NY,
             USA, 2000. ACM Press.

[KK02]   David Kempe and Jon M. Kleinberg. Protocols and impos-
             sibility results for gossip-based communication mechanisms.
             In *Proc. of the 43rd Symposium on Foundations of Computer
             Science (FOCS 2002)*, 2002.

[KKK+06]   Soon-Wook Kwon, Sung-Kyun Kwan, Jung-Yeol Kim, Hyun-Seok Yoo, and Moon-Young Cho. Wireless vibration sensor for tunnel construction. In *In Proc. of the 23rd International Symposium on Automation and Robotics in Construction (ISARC 2006)*, 2006.

[KMW04]   Fabian Kuhn, Thomas Moscibroda, and Roger Wattenhofer. Unit disk graph approximation. In *Proc. of the Joint Workshop on Foundations of Mobile Computing*, 2004.

[KPC+06]   Sukun Kim, Shamim Pakzad, David E. Culler, James Demmel, Gregory Fenves, Steve Glaser, and Martin Turon. Health monitoring of civil infrastructures using wireless sensor networks. Technical Report UCB/EECS-2006-121, EECS Department, University of California, Berkeley, Oct 2006.

[KW05]   Holger Karl and Andreas Willig. *Protocols and Architectures for Wireless Sensor Networks*. John Wiley & Sons, 2005.

[LBV06]   Koen Langendoen, Aline Baggio, and Otto Visser. Murphy loves potatoes: Experiences from a pilot sensor network deployment in precision agriculture. In *Proceedings of the 14th International Workshop on Parallel and Distributed Real-Time Systems (WPDRTS 2006)*, apr 2006.

[Lia02]   Weifa Liang. Constructing minimum-energy broadcast trees in wireless ad hoc networks. In *Proc. of the 3rd ACM Inter. Symposium on Mobile Ad Hoc Networking & Computing (MobiHoc 2002)*, 2002.

[LLWC03]   Philip Levis, Nelson Lee, Matt Welsh, and David Culler. TOSSIM: accurate and scalable simulation of entire tinyos applications. In *Proceedings of the 1st International Conference on Embedded Networked Sensor Systems (SenSys 2003)*, pages 126–137, New York, NY, USA, 2003. ACM.

[LMMR05]   Andreas Lachenmann, Pedro José Marrón, Daniel Minder, and Kurt Rothermel. An Analysis of Cross-Layer Interactions in Sensor Network Applications. In *Proceedings of the Second International Conference on Intelligent Sensors, Sensor Networks & Information Processing (ISSNIP 2005)*, pages 121–126, December 2005.

[LPCS04]   Philip Levis, Neil Patel, David Culler, and Scott Shenker. Trickle: A self-regulating algorithm for code propagation and maintenance in wireless sensor networks. In *Proceedings of*

Bibliography

the 1st conference on Symposium on Networked Systems Design and Implementation (NSDI 2004), pages 2–2, Berkeley, CA, USA, 2004. USENIX Association.

[LR03]   Koen Langendoen and Niels Reijers. Distributed localization in wireless sensor networks: a quantitative comparison. *Computer Networks*, 43(4):499–518, 2003.

[LRC+08]   Ren P. Liu, Zvi Rosberg, Iain B. Collings, Carol Wilson, Alex Y. Dong, and Sanjay Jha. Overcoming radio link asymmetry in wireless sensor networks. In *Proceedings of the 19th IEEE International Symposium on Personal, Indoor and Mobile Radio Communications (PIMRC 2008)*, Cannes, France, 2008.

[LWHS02]   Dan Li, Kerry D. Wong, Yu H. Hu, and Akbar M. Sayeed. Detection, classification, and tracking of targets. *IEEE Signal Processing Magazine*, 19(2):17–30, 2002.

[MBFM07]   Jonas Meyer, Reinhard Bischoff, Glauco Feltrin, and Masoud Motavalli. A Low Power Wireless Sensor Network for Structural Health Monitoring. In *Proceedings of the 3rd International Conference on Structural Health Monitoring of Intelligent Infrastructure*, 2007.

[MBSF06]   Jonas Meyer, Reinhard Bischoff, Olga Saukh, and Glauco Feltrin. A low power wireless sensor network for structural health monitoring. In *In Proc. of the 3rd International Conference on Bridge Maintenance (IABMAS 2006)*, 2006.

[MFHH02]   Samuel Madden, Michael J. Franklin, Joseph M. Hellerstein, and Wei Hong. TAG: A Tiny AGgregation service for ad-hoc sensor networks. *ACM SIGOPS Operating Systems Review*, 36(SI):131–146, 2002.

[MFHH05]   Samuel R. Madden, Michael J. Franklin, Joseph M. Hellerstein, and Wei Hong. TinyDB: An acquisitional query processing system for sensor networks. *ACM Transactions on Database Systems*, 30:122–173, 2005.

[MLM+04]   Pedro José Marrón, Andreas Lachenmann, Daniel Minder, Jörg Hähner, Kurt Rothermel, and Christian Becker. Adaptation and cross-layer issues in sensor networks. In *Proceedings of the First International Conference on Intelligent Sensors, Sensor Networks & Information Processing (ISSNIP 2004)*, pages 623–628, December 2004.

[MMLR05a]   Pedro José Marrón, Daniel Minder, Andreas Lachenmann, and Kurt Rothermel. TinyCubus: A flexible and adaptive cross-layer framework for sensor networks. In *4th GI/ITG KuVS Fachgespräch "Drahtlose Sensornetze"*, Technical Report TR 481, Computer Science Department, ETH Zurich, pages 49–54, March 2005.

[MMLR05b]   Pedro José Marrón, Daniel Minder, Andreas Lachenmann, and Kurt Rothermel. TinyCubus: An adaptive cross-layer framework for sensor networks. *it - Information Technology*, 47(2):87–97, 2005.

[MMLR05c]   Daniel Minder, Pedro José Marrón, Andreas Lachenmann, and Kurt Rothermel. Experimental construction of a meeting model for smart office environments. In *Proceedings of the First REALWSN 2005 Workshop on Real-World Wireless Sensor Networks, SICS Technical Report T2005:09*, June 2005.

[MOJ06]   Ar Milenkovic, Chris Otto, and Emil Jovanov. Wireless sensor networks for personal health monitoring: Issues and an implementation. *Computer Communications (Special issue: Wireless Sensor Networks: Performance, Reliability, Security, and Beyond)*, 29:2521–2533, 2006.

[MSKG05]   Pedro José Marrón, Olga Saukh, Markus Krüger, and Christian Große. Sensor network issues in the Sustainable Bridges project. In *European Projects Session of the Second European Workshop on Wireless Sensor Networks (EWSN 2005)*, January 2005.

[MSS97]   Masoud Mansouri-Samani and Morris Sloman. Gem: a generalized event monitoring language for distributed systems. *Distributed Systems Engineering*, 4(2):96–108, 1997.

[NOM]   Nomotida web-site. http://www.nomotida.net.

[OAVRH06]   ElMoustapha Ould-Ahmed-Vall, George F. Riley, and Bonnie S. Heck. Distributed fault-tolerance for event detection using heterogeneous wireless sensor networks. Technical report, Georgia Institute of Technology, 2006.

[PSC05]   Joseph Polastre, Robert Szewczyk, and David Culler. Telos: enabling ultra-low power wireless research. In *Proceedings of the 4th international symposium on Information processing* in sensor networks (IPSN 2005), page 48, Piscataway, NJ, USA, 2005. IEEE Press.

[Pul00]   Wendy Pullan. *Structure*. Cambridge: Cambridge University Press., 2000.

[QC06]   Lei Fang Tarek Abdelzaher John Stankovic Sang Son Qing Cao, Tian He. Efficiency centric communication model for wireless sensor networks. In *Proceedings of the 25th International Conference on Computer Communications (INFOCOM 2006)*, pages 1–12, Barcelona, Spain, April 2006.

[RFMB04]   Kay Römer, Christian Frank, Pedro José Marrón, and Christian Becker. Generic role assignment for wireless sensor networks. In *Proceedings of the 11th ACM SIGOPS European Workshop*, pages 7–12, Leuven, Belgium, September 2004.

[RLD+08]   Z. Rosberg, R.P. Liu, A. Dong, T. Le Dinh, and S. Jha. ARQ with Implicit and Explicit ACKs in Sensor Networks. In *IEEE Globecom 2008*, New Orleans, 2008.

[RM04a]   Kay Römer and Friedemann Mattern. The design space of wireless sensor networks. *IEEE Wireless Communications*, 11(6):54–61, December 2004.

[RM04b]   Kay Römer and Friedemann Mattern. Event-based systems for detecting real-world states with sensor networks: A critical analysis. In *DEST Workshop on Signal Processing in Sensor Networks at ISSNIP*, pages 389–395, Melbourne, Australia, December 2004.

[RPSS03]   Ananth Rao, Christos Papadimitriou, Scott Shenker, and Ion Stoica. Geographic routing without location information. In *Proc. of the 9th Int. Conf. on Mobile Computing and Networking*, 2003.

[Sav02]   Andreas Savvides. Design of a wearable sensor badge for smart kindergarten. In *Proceedings of the 6th IEEE International Symposium on Wearable Computers (ISWC 2002)*, page 231, Washington, DC, USA, 2002. IEEE Computer Society.

[SBAS04]   Nisheeth Shrivastava, Chiranjeeb Buragohain, Divyakant Agrawal, and Subhash Suri. Medians and beyond: new aggregation techniques for sensor networks. In *Proc. of the 2nd Inter. Conf. on Embedded Networked Sensor Systems*, 2004.

[SEN]   Sentilla web-site. http://www.sentilla.com/.

[Sha78]   Michael Ian Shamos. Computational geometry. PhD thesis, 1978.

[SHB⁺03]   Illya Stepanov, Jörg Hähner, Christian Becker, Jing Tian, and Kurt Rothermel. A meta-model and framework for user mobility in mobile networks. In *In Proc. of the 11th Inter. Conf. on Networking (ICON)*, 2003.

[SML⁺06]   Olga Saukh, Pedro José Marrón, Andreas Lachenmann, Matthias Gauger, Daniel Minder, and Kurt Rothermel. Generic Routing Metric and Policies for WSNs. In *Proceedings of the Third European Workshop on Wireless Sensor Networks (EWSN 2006)*, pages 99–114, February 2006.

[Sob05]   Joao Luís Sobrinho. An Algebraic Theory of Dynamic Network Routing. *IEEE/ACM Transactions on Networking*, 13(5):1160–1173, 2005.

[SSG⁺08]   Olga Saukh, Robert Sauter, Matthias Gauger, Pedro José Marrón, and Kurt Rothermel. On boundary recognition without location information in wireless sensor networks. In *Proceedings of the 2008 International Conference on Information Processing in Sensor Networks (IPSN 2008)*, pages 207–218, Washington, DC, USA, 2008. IEEE Computer Society.

[SSM08]   Olga Saukh, Robert Sauter, and Pedro José Marrón. Time-bounded and space-bounded sensing in wireless sensor networks. In *Proceedings of the 4th IEEE International Conference on Distributed Computing in Sensor Systems*, pages 357–371, 2008.

[SSMM08]   Olga Saukh, Robert Sauter, Jonas Meyer, and Pedro José Marrón. Motefinder: a deployment tool for sensor networks. In *REALWSN '08: Proceedings of the workshop on Real-world wireless sensor networks*, pages 41–45, New York, NY, USA, 2008. ACM.

[SW06]   Stefan Schmid and Roger Wattenhofer. Algorithmic Models for Sensor Networks. In *Proc. of the 14th Int. Workshop on Parallel and Distributed Real-Time Systems*, 2006.

[SY07]   Adam Silberstein and Jun Yang. Many-to-Many Aggregation for Sensor Networks. *Proceedings of the 23rd International*

Conference on Data Engineering (ICDE 2007), 0:986–995, 2007.

[tin]   Tinyos web-site. http://www.tinyos.net/.

[Tou83]   Godfried T. Toussaint. Solving geometric problems with the rotating calipers. In *Proc. of IEEE MELECON*, 1983.

[VBL07]   Chinh T. Vu, Raheem A. Beyah, and Yingshu Li. Composite event detection in wireless sensor networks. In *In Proc. of the IEEE International Performance, Computing, and Communications Conference*, 2007.

[WGM06]   Yue Wang, Jie Gao, and Joseph S.B. Mitchell. Boundary recognition in sensor networks by topological methods. In *Proc. of the 12th Int. Conf. on Mobile Computing and Networking*, 2006.

[WNE02]   Jeffrey E. Wieselthier, Gam D. Nguyen, and Anthony Ephremides. Energy-efficient broadcast and multicast trees in wireless networks. *Mobile Networks and Applications*, 7(6):481–492, 2002.

[WTC03]   Alec Woo, Terence Tong, and David Culler. Taming the underlying challenges of reliable multihop routing in sensor networks. In *Proceedings of the 1st International Conference on Embedded Networked Sensor Systems (SenSys 2003)*, pages 14–27, New York, NY, USA, 2003. ACM.

[XBO]   Crossbow web-site. http://www.xbow.com/.

[XRC$^+$04]   Ning Xu, Sumit Rangwala, Krishna Kant Chintalapudi, Deepak Ganesan, Alan Broad, Ramesh Govindan, and Deborah Estrin. A wireless sensor network for structural monitoring. In *Proceedings of the 2nd International Conference on Embedded Networked Sensor Systems (SenSys 2004)*, pages 13–24, New York, NY, USA, 2004. ACM.

[YS07]   Sunhee Yoon and Cyrus Shahabi. The clustered aggregation (CAG) technique leveraging spatial and temporal correlations in wireless sensor networks. *ACM Transactions on Sensor Networks*, 3:3, 2007.

[YW08]   Y. Yang and J. Wang. Design Guidelines for Routing Metrics in Multihop Wireless Networks. In *Proceedings of the 27th IEEE Conference on Computer Communications (INFOCOM 2008)*, pages 1615–1623, 2008.

[ZG03]   Jerry Zhao and Ramesh Govindan. Understanding Packet Delivery Performance in Dense Wireless Sensor Networks. In *Proceedings of the 1st International Conference on Embedded Networked Sensor Systems (SenSys 2003)*, pages 1–13, New York, NY, USA, 2003. ACM.

[ZHKS04]   Gang Zhou, Tian He, Sudha Krishnamurthy, and John A. Stankovic. Impact of Radio Irregularity on Wireless Sensor Networks. In *Proceedings of the 2nd International Conference on Mobile Systems, Applications, and Services (MobiSys 2004)*, pages 125–138, New York, NY, USA, 2004. ACM.

Bibliography